Reiki Vibrations
with
33 Guided Meditations and Affirmations

LaTanya L. Hill, JD, Reiki Master

Registered Holy Fire III Karuna Reiki Master

BookLocker
Saint Petersburg, Florida

Published by BookLocker.com, Inc., St. Petersburg, Florida.

Printed on acid-free paper.

BookLocker.com, Inc.
2021

First Edition

May the Creator send peace and blessings.

A special thanks to my family, friends, supporters, and clients. I hope you all achieve the best life offers at every moment. I will forever send you the highest Reiki healing.

-from my heart chakra to yours

Table of Contents

CHAPTER 1

<u>Origins</u>

When Reiki found me, I was already knowledgeable about the healing and spirit realm. But my experience didn't mean I knew everything. I still had lessons to learn. Some lessons were spiritual in nature, with internal work being the prime directive so that I could elevate in vibration. Whereas other lessons were instituted to teach me how to help people find their true path in this world. There were so many unusual circumstances of the spiritual nature. Circumstances I had not dealt with in the past, ones I did not know could happen in my life. The way these situations presented themselves led me to have lots of additional questions about Reiki and how it works with different people. So, I asked my questions. However, no one could properly answer me. The response was always, "meditate on it," or "listen to your Reiki." So, I did.

My inquisitive nature led me to testing Reiki. I ate lots of meat to see if it affected my channeling versus when I ate only fruits and vegetables. There was a slight lull in the energy with meat in my system. It is better to have light foods. I drank alcohol, got drunk, to see if Reiki would still flow. It did not. I had a very strong physical reaction of dizziness and nausea that only stopped when I turned off the flow of energy. I intentionally thought of negative things while channeling Reiki to see if it would stop. It did. Reiki only started again when I cleansed my mind. I noted these things and more to know Reiki like I know myself. I determined every action I did was a success in that respect.

It is from the testing, my meditations, and my working with Reiki that I received answers. By focusing and honing my skills to integrating Reiki into my physical and spiritual self, there was clarity. I now have reached a level where Reiki is as essential to me as breathing. Everything I do and say is derived from meditation and Reiki.

When I began teaching Reiki, I noticed that a lot of people who were healers had stopped practicing. Most had even forgotten the style they studied and the basics. This Reiki handbook is written to give you the essence of what is needed when starting your journey into energy healing. It is also a reminder for those who have neglected their Reiki gift but want to reconnect with it. It combines things you are not told in most certification classes with detailed meditations and affirmations to help guide you. Keep it close whenever you need an aide.

I truly hope my personal and professional story helps assist all Reiki healers and those persons interested in personal healing. As a refresher, let us begin with a very brief review of the history of Reiki.

Reiki is the Japanese technique for channeling Universal energy through the hands. Although people previously practiced Reiki in Japan for many years, it had become dormant until Dr. Mikao Usui, a Buddhist monk, began practicing and training others in the 1920s. Dr. Usui is known as the founder of Usui Reiki and given the honor of being the one to re-establish Reiki as a popular and effective healing method.

There are also a few legends about how Dr. Usui came to discover Reiki. One is of him injuring his foot on Mount Kurama and touching it with his hands to discover his injury healed, indicating the gift of Reiki being bestowed upon him. Another one is Dr. Usui undergoing a spiritual awakening on Mount Kurama wherein the information about Reiki was given to him from a higher source after fasting and meditation. It is not important which is correct or how it came to be. The fact is that through his dedication, knowledge and innovation, Dr. Usui re-established a method of intuitive communication and integration with spirit to help others heal.

To understand how Reiki came to America, we must learn about two of his prominent students, one being Dr. Chujiro Hayashi. Dr. Hayashi was a former naval officer who ascended to Master level, taught Reiki, and eventually opened healing clinics. He combined his medical background with Reiki and created hand positions for healers to use for certain illnesses. These hand positions improved Reiki by ensuring a comprehensive healing for clients. It also gave the novice healer or healers who are not comfortable with the intuitive method of Usui Reiki a written hand guide for healing. Dr. Hayashi also enhanced the Attunement process students undergo to channel energy, making it more precise and refined. As you can already tell, Reiki is a healing method that continually progresses.

This brings us to Mrs. Hawayo Takata, who was a Japanese-American resident of Hawaii visiting Japan. The story is that Mrs. Takata was extremely ill before leaving for Japan. While there, she sought treatment, but doctors were not able to assist her. She learned about the work of Reiki practitioners at a healing center in Tokyo, which happened to be owned by Dr. Hayashi, and went there for healing. Mrs. Takata received periodic treatment from the Reiki healers and was finally healed. This so impressed her, that she requested to be a student of Dr.

Hayashi. During her stay in Japan, she became a level 1 and level 2 Reiki healer.

Upon her return to Hawaii, Mrs. Takata continued practicing Reiki and sharing it with others. She kept in contact with Dr. Hayashi. When he visited Mrs. Takata in Hawaii, they continued her training, certifying her as a Reiki Master under his lineage. Not long after, Mrs. Takata began teaching Reiki in Hawaii at a price of $10,000 for most students. Mrs. Takata's teachings were verbal, no one was allowed to write anything. However, after her death, some of her pupils wrote her teachings in a manual to preserve the information and continue her legacy. They also lowered the exorbitant price Mrs. Takata charged to make Reiki accessible to more people.

This story has a few variations, but the point is that Mrs. Takata is the one who brought Reiki to the western world. Her respect for the teachings and love for the healing are still present and honored in our modern times. Today there are thousands of people practicing Reiki and millions who have tried it. It is considered complementary healthcare in America, with many hospitals offering it to patients. Multiple studies on the effectiveness of Reiki and how it helps people recover from surgery, relax, and heal faster have been conducted. All of this is in progress in the western world because of Mrs. Takata.

Reiki Defined

In breaking down the word Reiki, Rei means "God's wisdom or the higher power," and Ki means "life force energy." So, combined, we know the energy that is transferred is "God energy." This energy is a cognizant energy that is guided spiritually to help a person relax, remove stress, recover from emotional trauma, and so much more. Reiki is typically practiced in-person using a method of "hands-on," "hands-off," or a combination of the two. There is no touching of private areas on a person's body. A Reiki healer can also send healing by Distant/Remote Reiki through use of an electronic device, such as a computer, or by simply "connecting" with the person spiritually. This "connecting" is accomplished by multiple methods. The first is imagining the person in front of you and sending Reiki to the parts of the body directed by your spirit. You may also connect by picturing the person in one of your hands and sending Reiki. And finally, you may use a stuffed animal to represent the person to send healing energy to all blocked areas.

Be aware that the energy being channeled is a conscious and knowing energy that only works for the best for each person. It cannot do harm to anyone and may not be used for bad intentions. It will help a person in every beneficial way possible. The only condition is that the person must accept the healing energy offered from the Universe. Once the person accepts and is open to healing, Reiki healers channel the energy down from the Universe through the physical body of the Reiki healer to the body of the client. When this occurs, there is a removal of negative energy. This removal allows the proper flow of positive energy through the chakras, energy points, and energy channels within and above the body, resulting in its natural ability to self-heal. Reiki can also cleanse the energy body and aura to aid in the healing flow of energy points and channels on and within the body.

The healing that takes place can be physical, emotional, mental, spiritual, or a mix of the aforementioned. Sometimes, what could seem like a physical ailment or pain within the body is a strong emotional memory from a significant incident in life that the client has buried deep inside. Reiki will assist the person by bringing forth any negative emotions so the person may acknowledge them and heal.

Because Reiki healers only channel conscious energy, it knows what is needed to assist a person in a session. Sometimes a client will want to work on a specific issue. This can be accomplished, but Reiki will also go to where there are more serious issues to remove them from the person's physical and spiritual body. This does not mean that the client's request will not be completed. It means that Reiki can do multiple things at once and be in more than one place as it heals. Reiki wants the best for all of us because it is a part of us. Therefore, as mentioned, it will always work for the good in every way possible.

Consider this, since humans and everything around is composed of energy, Reiki energy is extending help to its own Universal being. For instance, picture the Universe as a giant body identical to yours. You can think of the planets as the organs and the natural elements grown on each as cells, ligaments, tissue, etc., with our consciousness as space. When we are not functioning properly, even if it is one of us, the Universal body detects this anomaly and wants to fix it because we are all one energetically. The Universal body will do its best to heal the ailment and correct the problem so that it may function at the highest level. But since we are living cells with a spiritual body of our own and free will, it cannot clear away anything without our approval. We are an independent planet orbiting in our own atmosphere within our space body. This is the knowing part of Reiki. It understands that although we are one with it, we still have our own choice to exist as we so choose, whether the existence chosen is negative or positive. Therefore, Reiki needs the person to want help so that the Universal body functions well. Simply put, we are integral to the health of the Universe because it is integrated into us.

The Reiki Healer

Be aware that there is not a special requirement needed for a person to become a Reiki healer. We are all born with the ability, but not everyone is interested or able to open up to receive the connection. All one needs is an open mind and being receptive to the gift of Reiki. If that happens, the Reiki healer will undergo a process, guided by a Reiki Master Teacher, to receive Attunements, which are also called Placements, and called Ignitions at the higher level. This process means that the person's energy system and chakras become open and elevated in vibration to receive and channel Universal energy. For those persons who are interested and want to learn Reiki for self-healing or to heal others, there are three different levels you should know, level 1 Reiki Practitioner, level 2 Reiki Practitioner, and Reiki Master/Reiki Master Teacher.

A person certified as a level 1 Reiki Practitioner uses Reiki for self-healing and does not receive symbols to enhance the healing. The person also cannot open a Reiki healing business at this level. This is a beginning stage, and the energy channeled may not be as strong as the higher levels, even if a person has innate gifts that combine with Reiki to strengthen it. What could happen is the person might end up using their own energy in a healing session, which can cause the person to become fatigued or take on the energy of others. This contradicts one of the main reasons for getting the Attunement and becoming certified, which is to not use innate energy, only Universal energy. That way, there is no subliminal coercion or tainting of the energy being sent out. It remains God's energy, pure and beneficial.

If you are a level 1 Reiki Practitioner who works on others to enhance your channeling or to assist in healing, be cognizant of the energy level used and how your body feels afterward. Reiki does not tire you out. It strengthens and heals you while you are helping others. If you become tired, more than likely your energy is being used with Reiki or alone. To help you remove yourself from the healing, focus on remaining neutral when using Reiki. Keep all your emotions, thoughts, and beliefs out of the session. Practice using the energy in different personal situations to learn more about it. Constant use allows a person to move up in vibration, which results in an understanding of how to properly use Reiki with better channeling ability of the energy.

As a level 2 Reiki Practitioner, a person can channel more energy and receive symbols to help enhance the energy to target certain mental, emotional, spiritual, and physical issues. A level 2 Reiki Practitioner and above can open a business and practice as a professional healer. There is also a deeper understanding of the energy based on the teachings and practice. A person learns how Reiki works not only in a person's everyday life but also in past and future lives. The caution about combining your energy in a session with a client that was given for level 1 Reiki Practitioners holds true for Level 2. Always remain a clean channel for the energy. After a certain amount of time, most level 2 Reiki Practitioners want to delve even deeper and become a Reiki Master.

A Reiki Master or Reiki Master Teacher offers a person a higher level of channeling ability. There are additional symbols with stronger enhancing ability for specific issues and an intimate understanding of how the energy and symbols may combine. This level of training teaches Reiki benefits to the person on multiple planes of existence. There is also the ability to handle more complicated issues on a spiritual level and a significant increase in the person's ability to raise their own vibration and the vibration of others. A Reiki Master Teacher can do all the plus teach others and attune them to the Universal energy on all three levels of certification.

I am blessed to be a Reiki Master Teacher in my styles of Reiki, which allows me to assist others in opening the path to Reiki. I have been able to certify and train in-person and remotely, both being effective in the Attunement process. I am a traditionalist in that I keep to the standards I learned in my certification classes from level 1 Reiki up to Master Teacher. However, I believe in my students getting lots of practice using the energy in class and encourage them to never turn off their Reiki. Also, because of my innate gifts, I focus a lot on students discovering their own spiritual gift and using it with their Reiki to help them in life. I love teaching others Reiki and seeing how the energy works with each student. It is a divine gift to show others the path of light and goodness in this world.

Reiki Styles

There are many styles and schools teaching Reiki. I will not list them here because, at my last count, there were over 22 styles of Reiki. If you are not a Reiki healer or someone who wants to learn another style, I recommend researching and meditating on which is more in alignment with your individual spirit. I have met people who have created their own style of healing by combining what they have learned or receiving spiritual guidance to create new symbols and new methods. I believe it's wonderful that Reiki still progresses, just like the days of Dr. Hayashi and Mrs. Takata.

As for me, I chose to study and be certified in a style that was in alignment with my spiritual beliefs, Holy Fire III® and Karuna® Reiki. After each certification, I practiced the required six months until I finally became a Registered Holy Fire III® Karuna® Reiki Master Teacher. Holy Fire and Karuna Reiki are styles divinely created and subsequently trademarked by William Rand, founder of the International Center for Reiki Training. This Reiki is so powerful. I knew with my first placement that I was correct in my choice. It integrated with my natural empathic and prophetic gifts, which amplified my healing abilities. I want to mention that although my natural gifts are mixed with healing, it is still not my energy being used. My natural gifts are channeled to the Universe, then this personal energy is enhanced with Reiki and channeled back to me with physical confirmation, such as messages. If you experience messages with your Reiki, keep your personal thoughts, opinions, and ideas out of any received. The best thing to do is deliver the message, as you hear it, with no supposition. A client will know what it means, even if they do not want to admit it or immediately recognize it. Remember, practicing Reiki requires that we honor and respect. Let the Universe show you the best Reiki style as you begin your journey to help heal others.

CHAPTER 2

<u>IMREIKINOW</u>

We are all born with special gifts. Yet when we come into this world, it is as if the spirit within has forgotten how to connect with the Universal energy that helps strengthen and hone our spiritual abilities. To make it worse, it seems as if the body subjugates the knowledge further as it matures and becomes indoctrinated into the material world and society's systemic beliefs. But there is always a Universal knocking on the door that comes to all of us. For some, it is a tragic event in life, such as an illness, an accident, or even a death of a loved one. For others, it is a gnawing sense of being incomplete and disconnected from society. Whatever occurs is intimate and specific to that person. No one else will understand the meaning, nor should they.

This can be a frightening moment, especially when the person realizes it means releasing most, if not all, of the beliefs held from childhood until that time. The realization that all thoughts, hopes, and dreams belong to someone else is overwhelming. However, the benefits that come by walking through the door and creating a new world more than make up for any fear experienced. There is a sense of freedom that takes over and refocuses the person's perspective about life. The introspection required allows the person to find hidden parts of themselves, whether good or bad. The acceptance that takes place of both parts moves the person one step closer to full spiritual integration with the Universe. Barriers to connectedness disintegrate as the Universal energy moves closer to that person's spirit, allowing locked away memories to surface and negative ones to heal. The idea of being something bigger than the individual self turns into a strong desire to explore and discover, leading to higher levels of spiritual attainment. The person becomes an authentic self with independent thoughts and beliefs. The unconscious mimicry has left.

For me, I have always been in the spirit realm ever since I was a child. But like most, as I grew up, I put my gifts to the side. Instead of practicing and strengthening them, I integrated and assimilated with the world system. I didn't want to be different. I stood out enough with being an African-American female and not the stereotypical one at that, so blending helped me. At least, that was what I thought. However, my spirit was and is of the kind that refused to allow me to relax unless I am doing spiritual work. It needed to reconnect to its larger self, the Universe. Therefore, when my time came, I opened the door, each one of them. I did not care what I found on the other side. I decided to face whatever Angel appeared, whether it be one of peace or one of chaos. My spirit was intent on waking up.

Meditation and prayer helped me on my journey to realize my true self. In meditation, my spirit found the first few levels of reconnecting with what was forgotten at birth, the Universal source. And yet, I still believed there was something I needed, something missing. I continued to meditate and pray until I received the gift of seeing how we are all connected, how everything living and non-living is, as scientists say, simply energy. By this I mean, when I open my eyes, I see miniscule, fluorescent pink, white, blue, and yellow lights on everything. I have always seen this and believed everyone saw the world this way. It was only recently that I was informed only a small amount of people see the connected energy. I think that is a shame because if you can see where everything and everyone is connected, you begin to look for similarities instead of differences. When you look for similarities, you understand people better and get along better. When you look for differences, you alienate and disconnect, causing separation. Let's all try to look for the similarity so we can establish a connection and have a more peaceful life.

Back to my point, this was not the only thing that led me to where I am now. This was the impetus, a small door opening to prepare me for what was about to come. The genuine request from the Universe to reconnect arrived in the form of illness. My physical body betrayed me, breaking down. I was overworking myself at my job and in my personal life. I was extremely stressed out and so invested in this material world that I had become sick. I was always medicated to alleviate pain. It took many doctors to misdiagnose me. I struggled at work, with people, with being me. There was intermittent pain and inflammation in my heart and throughout my body. At times, it was so strong all I wanted was to leave this world. I could not see living a life where I could not walk, sleep, or dress myself without excruciating pain. And with all this, I still had to go to work. I don't come from a wealthy family. I had to make my own way in this world. No matter how I suffered, no matter how much pain I was in that day, I had to show up. I worked, even if for a few hours, to get assignments completed so that I may pay life expenses. I was in constant agony, could not breathe properly, and no one believed the gravity of the situation because I looked healthy. I felt like I had to continue with no time for me to heal. I was in a very low vibration.

This primary world function, to keep going no matter what, was foremost in my mind. It distracted me from my spiritual self. I was detaching from my meditations, my prayers, and connection to the other world. I couldn't hear my spirit speaking to me anymore. At the time, I was regularly attending church, but it didn't matter. I was at the most basic of needs, survival in this material world, so spirit was diminishing.

One day, this woman and I began talking at church. She told me about her sister who had similar issues. Medical professionals had even relegated her sister to a wheelchair because of the pain. But due to her doctor in San Diego, she was now climbing mountains. Of course, I got the name of the specialist, who ended up saving my life too. If not for him, I would have continued to be misdiagnosed and probably transitioned into the spirit world by now. You wouldn't be reading this handbook and I would not be here to help so many people with Reiki.

It was because of his expertise and thorough exams that a proper diagnosis of Rheumatic Fever occurred. He took me off all the pills and integrated holistic medicine as part of my regularly prescribed treatment. This refocused my mind, body, and spirit. I began to meditate again while undergoing treatment. I could hear my spirit clearer once he took away the medications and the effects left my system. I heard my spirit whispering to me to heal myself. My hands moved to the parts of my body that were in the most pain, relieving the hurt. This became my routine, to breathe, to meditate, and to heal myself in between treatments. Throughout this process, I learned control, connection to spirit, and understood that this world is not to be my focus. By being ill, I became stronger in my spiritual beliefs and more connected with Divinity.

As I healed with one condition, a previous condition flared up which resulted in two unsuccessful surgeries. I was off work recovering and focusing on healing myself for this new situation. I prayed and meditated daily. There was a part of me that knew there was more to learn and that I could do better. Then one night, I asked for a teacher who could properly teach me healing.

The next morning, I woke up and heard in my mind, 'You need to learn Reiki.' I had never heard of Reiki, so I looked it up online. Once I read about it and realized what it was, it shocked me that I didn't know because I had been doing healing my entire life. I had no idea people had businesses focused on healing or that they were being taught how to do it. Healing for me was natural while growing up. Once again, the Universal energy turned my perspective in the right direction, showing me a path where I could create another life for myself. I signed up for training and certification to become an Usui Holy Fire III Reiki Practitioner II. Once I received my placements for Reiki, all spiritual doors opened for me. I used Reiki, not my energy, while still undergoing treatment to help heal myself. The change in results was immediate and strong. After six months, I was in good health all around and no longer needed treatment or surgeries for my conditions. This prompted me to start my own energy healing business, IMREIKINOW®. I researched, created a logo with my personal tagline, trademarked everything, and published my website, www.imreikinow.com, within six months. I was officially in business to help others be their best and most authentic selves.

The name of my business derived from what I believed and knew would be a new life for me because of what Reiki did to help heal me. Reiki didn't just physically remove pain from my body and alleviate my symptoms. It helped me to be at peace, be more understanding, and still be able to stand up for myself positively, filled with love, not anger, or hate. There was no longer stress and strife in my life. My focus was on being happy and healthy, no matter what. The world was different for me.

As I grew in Reiki and Reiki grew inside me, my spiritual gifts became stronger and more effective. I also had better control over unpleasant situations and my mental and emotional state. Reiki cleared away all my old fears, regrets, insecurities, and anger. For some people, the clearing from an Attunement may be a pleasant and silent release, maybe crying and an awareness of being lighter. But in my case, I had a tingling sensation all over my body, a debilitating headache, and body aches. I became fatigued and could not move for a few hours. I even had extreme extrasensory experiences, such as prophetic dreams and the sensation of someone holding my hand or my foot. There was a period where my eyes had calcium deposits coming out of them, which made my vision different in that everything seemed brighter and more colorful than before. Both eyes also had a moment where I could not see out of the eye because the light of day was so intense. The sun was so bright, it pained my eye, so I had to wear shades, even inside, if I wanted to keep my eye open. This lasted about two days for each eye. Anyone else would have been scared, but I was elated. I understood that with Reiki, my body was becoming more. After each cleansing experience, I was a new person. Whatever did not serve my higher purpose was lifted away while something special was simultaneously added.

This new person I became wanted to keep moving up in vibration, to learn more. So, I became an Usui Holy Fire III Reiki Master. It was during that certification that I realized how much energy could flow through my body and how Reiki had altered me for the best. At some point, my vibrational level began to raise on its own. I didn't have to "upgrade" as they taught me in class. But also, the world and its people were different. It was like looking inside a kaleidoscope of varying colors, shapes, and sizes of spiritual entities moving around in flesh, each on varying levels of understanding.

I never doubted the flow of Reiki because it gave me physical manifestations from the beginning. I knew the energy moved around and through me because of a slight inflammation in my nasal passages, a tingling sensation moving through my hands and across my body, there was a numbness in my left thigh or left shoulder blade. There were even times when the surrounding temperature would change, and a cool breeze combined with the sweet smell of flowers would flow around me.

These ethereal experiences made me want to channel more energy for the highest level of healing. I wanted to push myself to the extreme point, to see how much energy can flow through one body to heal and help others in this world. I meditated on the approach best used to achieve my purpose and, as before, my spirit directed me to become a Karuna Reiki Master as well. As always, my spirit was correct and led me to a perfect outcome. Now, I am in a state of healing myself and others without thought. The symbols that I learned are a part of me and in sessions, the energy knows when to move from Holy Fire to Karuna without my requesting. I always say that for me, Holy Fire energy is like a hand reaching inside and pulling out all the unneeded things that are holding on and bonding to the person; whereas Karuna is like a surgeon's knife removing the tiniest bits of the unneeded parts accumulated throughout life. I don't even know how I lived without Reiki now that we are one. I can even sense the energy moving throughout my body when I am sleeping. It never stops and I don't want it to leave, ever.

I'm sure my life's journey to Reiki is like most of you who find yourselves in this amazing field of energy healing. We had to shed our perception of what it means to live in this world and in this time. As energy healers, we understand the barriers that need to be removed to become our authentic selves. We also know that meditation is one of the best ways to help us hear our spiritual self, receive messages, and clear away those barriers. Even as I am writing this, the energy is moving around me, a cool whirlwind with feather like touches on my back and face. There is a sweetness in the air, as if someone has brought me a bouquet. This is what it is like to be a Reiki healer, to honestly and completely work with energy. It is beautiful and strong.

I hope my sharing my Reiki journey helps with understanding that once we begin this path, nothing ever looks the same as before. Even if you stop practicing, it is still there waiting with the door open. Walk through once more and join the rest of us in healing. Become IMREIKINOW.

CHAPTER 3

<u>Reiki Healing</u>

I touched upon some things I experienced with Reiki in the prior sections. Now, I will go into specifics so that you understand how unique Reiki is when properly practiced. It is true that other energy healers are tapping into the same energy and using similar methods to heal others. But my spirit sent me to Reiki, a special type of healing method in which you truly need nothing else with it, not stones, not incense, not feathers, not cards, nothing except cleansing and purifying yourself so that the energy may properly flow. Reiki only requires you to be your true higher self. The symbols we receive are spiritually given so that we may learn the true language that guides this Universe. They are integrated within our energy body and become one with us. Therefore, we, as healers, Reiki ourselves every day to release negative energy, raise our vibration, communicate with our Universal spirit, and to assist with the symbol integration process.

Now, let's discuss the session itself. In a healing session, all clients should set their intentions in advance or a moment before you begin. Your client may sit or lie down, fully clothed. Focal points are the chakras, major and minor, and any other energetic points on the body. You, as the healer, may perform "hands-on" or "hands-off" or a combination of the two methods in the session. If touching, you must ask first and know that it is not appropriate to touch a client on any intimate area, even if permission is granted for such. For those intimate places, hover your hands above the chakra or energy point at least three inches or more. The healing will be just as strong, touching or not. I do not touch my clients anymore unless they request it. My method is to hover my hands above the areas that need healing and send energy to the body. I rarely ask about touching because of this even if I know the client will not mind if touching is involved in the healing. As mentioned, it is a choice that you both should decide prior to beginning the session.

In this present time, we are recovering from a pandemic that prevented touching and gathering of people. The world was in isolation. This changed the way energy healers performed the majority of their work. There were no in-person sessions allowed. But Reiki is versatile. Another alternative, Distant Reiki, which is also called Remote Reiki, was performed. This is where you use the Distant symbol to connect with the person located in another place while conducting the healing session. This has become a very popular method during the pandemic and is effective in the same manner as an in-person session. A lot of Reiki healers I know did not want to use this form of healing at first, including me. This is because they taught us to sense the energy in person, not remotely. We also practiced more in-person Reiki, not Remote Reiki. But those healers, I included, have become quite proficient and prefer the unlimited access Remote Reiki offers healers and clients. You can be in England or Germany, and I can give you a healing session from my home in California. Reiki healers are universal and international.

When you are first starting out as a healer, it takes time to build confidence in sending Reiki over a distance. However, once you obtain assurance, there is no limitation to what may be achieved in a healing session. I recommend that Distant Reiki be practiced as soon as possible to help build self-esteem and learn the different physical reactions from clients and yourself.

When conducting a session, the procedural part is up to the healer and their spirit guide. Some healers work in silence with music playing in the background, while others like to question and explain what is occurring. Some healers use the visualizations and the symbols that were taught to them in class. While other healers add more personal things to their sessions, such as stones, crystals, and incense. Although additional items are not needed with Reiki, everyone individually grows, so what is done one day in a session may not be done another time. If it leads to good healing, all Reiki methods is fine and well.

Personally, Reiki led me to use unique healing visualizations. During a session, there is a strong connection being built between the physical and spiritual world. Guided visualizations help a client to focus and relax. For some people, it is easier to open and clear chakras within and around the body when using visualizations. I have discovered it assists a person's spirit to communicate about areas that need healing and why. There is also an increase in energy due to the openness initiated, which helps teach me and my client how to sense the energy flowing for a particular issue. I have been told by clients that dormant emotions and memories that held them back were acknowledged and released because of my guided visualizations. Therefore, the effectiveness is without question. I have faith that you will also figure out what works for you and helps your clients heal better.

I also like to give my clients homework to help them prolong the healing. Therefore, every visualization I give in session is spiritually chosen for that person to use during personal meditation. It is also my way to teach my client how to connect with the higher self when not in session with me. I have mentioned previously how I have used meditation to assist me in my life's journey. I am a strong believer that it should be recommended by every energy healer to a client.

As we know, meditation itself is a strong spiritual practice that also focuses on healing. Through meditation, a person can learn to communicate with their spirit and the Universe. With this link, a person can seek answers to life's questions to understand the physical house where the spirit resides in a more comprehensive manner. Once this occurs, it leads to control over the inner processes that are stimulated by negative influences from the outside world.

Meditation can also be another way to perform physical inner healing. Guided visualizations fit perfectly with meditation, just as they do with Reiki. For instance, if a person's mental and emotional state are in constant moments of fear, anxiety, or stress, it causes a weakness of the spiritual body. This weak energy flows into the physical form, decreasing the immune system, creating a perfect scenario for illness to manifest and consume the healthy life force of an individual. To prevent this, the person should combine intermittent Reiki healing sessions with daily personal meditations even if the meditation is only ten minutes of solitude or quiet time to start. Reiki, mingled with meditation, is a positive integrative approach that strengthens the person on every level. This helps keep the good energy flowing, which longer allays the physical ailments brought about by negativity.

CHAPTER 4

My Reiki Sessions

As a Reiki Practitioner, I wanted to practice on everyone, young, old, disabled, healthy, stressed, happy; all were welcome. I requested in meditation to be shown signs that my Reiki was flowing because I wanted to prove to others that I knew what I was doing; that my Reiki was genuine. Due to this request, the physical manifestations of a slight inflammation in my nasal passages, numbing on my left thigh, featherlike sensations on my body, cool air surrounding me, and a sweet scent in the air whenever I channeled energy remained with me after my placements. As previously mentioned, I also received messages and phrases regarding the person's physical condition of which I could not be aware of in advance. Let me be clear when I say that I would not know in advance. I did not and do not ask my clients to tell me any information ahead of time.

I did this to keep the session pure and because I knew that if I had advance knowledge, people could explain away anything the Universe told me to help the person. I also wanted to make certain I kept my personal opinions and beliefs out of the session. Though I must admit, at one point I tried to collect information in advance to keep records, but I never looked at the five or six client information sheets I collected during that brief time. It seemed wrong to even collect information like that, so I stopped as soon as I started. I found another way to keep track of clients by documenting the events in my sessions afterwards. The benefit of that was that anyone who received healing from me knew that the energy was real and that nothing was fake or imagined by them or guessed by me.

For example, in one of my first client sessions, an impromptu session with a female in her mid 40s, I received my first spiritual message. My client was in a sitting position as I moved my hands above her main chakras and a few secondary chakras. I heard a voice say, 'Be careful of the knees.' This message continued throughout the session and whenever my hand moved to her knees, I noticed a bump of fiery energy balled up and the message became stronger. I could perceive the imbalance and heat spots on her body through my hands, and even on my person. I kept focusing Reiki on her knees until I didn't sense the energy flowing from my hands anymore.

When we finished, I requested she open her eyes and tell me how the session was for her. She stated she felt the energy pass through her body and move something out.

She also mentioned that she felt intense relaxation. I told her about the message regarding her knees. She admitted she had begun a new workout routine which had injured her knee. She had stopped for a few days so it could heal, but planned to begin again. It shocked her that I knew that since we never had a conversation. She was the first to tell me I had a gift. I thanked her for the compliment and reminded her to be careful of her knees. This session brought instant confirmation that no matter what, when it is time to help heal, the energy will show up. This was also the first Reiki session that showed me how Reiki would integrate with my innate gifts. It helped to build my confidence and my reputation.

Another client, a female in her late 40s, asked for a session so she could experience Reiki. She was interested in energy healing, but never had the opportunity or courage to go to a healer. During the Byosen scan, an initial scan to determine areas on the body that have blockages, I noticed a bundle of hot energy in her solar plexus and sacral chakras. I mentally heard a message, 'Something is wrong with the stomach.' As the healing proceeded, the message changed to, 'No, not the stomach, the intestines.' The phrase continued in my mind until I mentioned it to her during the session. She said nothing, and her face remained neutral. Throughout the session, I received other messages about her family. I made sure to relay the words exactly as I heard them.

Once the session was over, she hesitantly confirmed all the family messages. Once she confessed a few incidents, she realized the places she felt a release in her body were those holding negative emotions and perspectives. She also confirmed the phrase about her intestines. It ended up that she had a history of pain in that area. She had gone to the doctor and was using holistic herbs as part of her medical treatment to help resolve the problem. She asked me what she could do to ease her issues. As Reiki healers, we do not diagnose or prescribe medicine nor do anything that could be considered practicing medicine. I referred her back to her medical providers.

She and I worked together a few times after that. I taught her grounding methods and affirmations for meditation practice. This experience showed me how emotions can cause blockages that skew a person's perceptions so strongly, it creates physical pain that cannot be easily diagnosed. With that being said, Reiki is a great integrative approach with western medicine. I recommend it to everyone.

Reiki is also a wonderful impetus to help people hone and rediscover their own inner gifts. There was a female client in her early 30s who came to me with prophetic gifts that had yet to be discovered. Her session was an hour of peace and positive energy circulating all around. She and I both sensed other beings in the room with us. The air became chilly. There were vibrations of energy moving between us two. There was a feather-like sensation brushing against my face and moving up my arms. When the session was over, she recalled seeing her guides and family members who had transitioned. She said her third eye opened and powerful energy moved through her crown chakra downwards throughout her body. She told me she saw different colors of light and a bright white light around the room. It was a pleasure to give her a session.

Later that week, she informed me she could now remember her dreams, some of which had become true. I reminded her of the session and our discussion about her potential to have prophetic abilities, especially when she dreams. I don't know if she believed me at first, but once it happened, she was persuaded and happy about it. She had thought that she was going crazy because of her having a heightened sixth-sense, and that no one would believe the things she envisioned. Now, she realizes it is a gift from the Universe and I hope she uses her gift to create beautiful music.

Most people with whom I have worked all have a unique experience. I have found that in the same way as your fingerprint differs from everyone, so is Reiki with the person and the healer. Even when I have a session with someone, I do not know how it will speak to me regarding my client. I only know that my spirit will connect with the other person's spirit as a doorway for the energy, but my energy remains away from it all. From experience, I understand why healers should not place their energy in the sessions. It is not only because the person is in a suggestive state but also because that person can contaminate the healer as well. Therefore, you must follow protocol to use symbols and Reiki for protection, to cleanse the space, and to detach when the session terminates.

One client story to illustrate this point is when I was conducting Remote Reiki on a male in his late 40s who was knowledgeable about energy healing. As we were in the session, my spirit opened the door for Reiki by requesting his spirit to comply. There was an affirmative response, but throughout the session, I could sense his spirit hovering over my physical form. It was as if it was watching everything I was doing and taking notes or checking off a list. I requested it be at peace and it appeared to relax. In seconds, a surge of energy attempted to break through my protective shield and go for my third eye. It was like tentacles reaching out, causing a little pain. I detached it from me quickly and requested my

Angels and Jesus' energy to stand before me so it could attach to them. Once completed, the pain went away in seconds, and I could focus on channeling energy without having to block his energy from snooping around. Now, this may appear to be a malevolent attack, but it was not. It was his spirit seeking knowledge and reaching out to see who and what I was. It was performed without the man's conscious awareness or approval, like an automatic reaction.

When the session was over, I told him about the experience, in addition to the other information I received, such as visions of him taking notes and watching everything people do. I mentioned that there was a boss like energy emitting from him. He confirmed everything. He owned his own company, and he had that particular type of personality. What was more interesting to me was that he stated a shaman had informed him that his spirit was a strong one that "sought" other spirits. I interpreted this seeking as an attempt to overpower.

This client typifies why a Reiki healer must learn how to use Reiki in every manner possible, elevate in vibration, and keep a protective shield up at all times. There cannot be one second where any part of the healer's energy enters the healing process. Keep the door to your inner self closed and protected. Remain a conduit and hold the space for the God energy to come through. If a healer does not know how to remove a spiritual attachment or block an attachment, that person should keep practicing on family and friends before venturing out to strangers. Be aware that until that client is in session, you do not know the strength of the spirit it contains or of the protectors it has around it. Spirits can sometimes be dormant until something, like energy healing, awakens them.

Another type of client is the one who has a physical ailment, be it terminal or temporary. As mentioned, the thing to remember is that we are not medical professionals. Therefore, we cannot legally make promises to remove illness in these situations. We can only say that Reiki will help the person relax and release stress, which aids in healing. Though not listed in this book, there are a lot of studies online that show positive results of using Reiki during treatments to help alleviate pain. I am living proof of this. However, in the end, it is the desire of the person and God's plan that decides the outcome.

One client of mine, a man in his late 20s, had debilitating aftereffects from Covid-19, such as shortness of breath and body pain. He sought a Reiki session because he understood the scientific data of energy healing. A person might say he was a professor of such information. To continue my point, we had a Remote Reiki session in which I went through his chakras for clearing and gave him a guided meditation. I heard the phrase, 'It's in his childhood,' repeating over and over.

When we completed the session, he informed me that his breathing was better. He stated he could once again move a joint in his body that illness had prevented him from moving. Once we disconnected, I kept hearing the phrase about his childhood, so I sent him a message informing him of such. It ends up he was undergoing a childhood discovery that affected his emotional state. He had kept it confidential because of the severity of the situation. I did not ask for more details because it was not my place since I am only a conduit and messenger for the Universe when this occurs. As always, I recommended he use the meditations from the session to assist him on his journey, and we discussed that topic no more. We had two more sessions after that for different issues. With the last session, his energy was balanced and healthy. He was even thinking about becoming a Reiki healer. I hope he does, whether he asks me to teach him or not.

Another client was a female in her late 50s who was experiencing an itching sensation in her left foot that only occurred while she slept at night. The moment she mentioned it to me, I heard, 'It's emotional pain,' in my mind. As I performed the session, the phrase continued. Once I reached her left leg, there was a bump of hot energy that caused light pain in my hands, as if someone was pricking me with a needle. I relayed the phrase to her while channeling energy around the area until the needle like sensation in my hands went away.

Afterwards, she told me at the time I relayed the phrase, she had visions of her father and mother getting a divorce and him leaving the family. At that same moment, she said she experienced something release from her. She stated that there was a sweetness in the air prior to and during the session. She also described smelling a strong human body scent, then sweetness again. For clarity, I do not wear perfume or anything that would emit odor during sessions. I do this because I never know if a person has an allergy. Additionally, I did not personally experience a change of smell in the air that time, though I had in previous sessions with various clients.

For me, the sweetness is the presence of Angels, good energy. The human scent is the release of negative material energy. This session showed that not all blockages or stale energy within the body manifests by pain or illness or unpleasant emotions. Sometimes, it can be something as simple as an annoying itch that disturbs your sleep at night for no reason or an odor surrounding the body. It is good to pay attention to everything when we are in our healing sessions. Every moment is one of learning for all.

My last client story, an elderly female in her 60s, is another example of why we have to be clear with expectations when it comes to physical ailments. This was someone with a terminal illness. Reiki was used to help ease the pain and prepare my client for whatever the Universe and she decided would occur with her life. We had regular sessions scheduled after her treatments every month.

The focal point of her sessions, besides alleviating the symptoms, was to balance her emotional and mental state during her illness and treatment. If anyone knows someone who has a terminal illness, you understand the highs and lows that person experiences which can be detrimental to treatment and recovery. In this situation, I used few guided meditations. Instead, I allowed her body and mind to rest and remember what it was like to be healthy and young. To do that, we set her intentions with good thoughts that encompassed those ideas along with acceptance of her condition. We also had full-on, in-depth conversations while I gave her Reiki. I let her discuss anything that she wanted and if her conversation moved to death or anything of darkness, I inserted light and life into the exchange. This continued for over a year, and it was always a joy to see her. Although the illness continued, the pain lessened because she had accepted it as a part of her. She fought until she decided it was time to transition.

When I was told that she passed, there was minimal surprise. In our last sessions, her spirit had seemed ready to leave, even though her body seemed to look healthier. Her conversations were of agreement with life and how she lived. She was at peace with everything. She was and is a beautiful person, spirit, and soul. I know without a doubt that our sessions helped her to prepare for her new life while releasing some of the pain in this one. Reiki is about inner healing, but one thing we cannot change is our timeline here on Earth.

There are many other stories I could relay about my clients that could prove the effectiveness of Reiki and energy healing, but we Reiki healers already know and believe. The stories above are situations to be aware of in your own practice for those who are new and a reminder to those who have forgotten. The primary aim in a session is to help the client release negative energy and blockages so that the body can heal itself. These obstructions may consist of childhood trauma, illness, physical injury, mental or emotional trauma, or spiritual attachments. The healing may range from physical release or spiritual agreement. We must be prepared for anything and everything in this field of healing.

As mentioned before, negative energy can integrate within the system and create a blockage that prevents the flow of positive energy in the body. In order to maintain a healthy physical, mental, and emotional state, we need this good energy flowing within our energetic channels at all times. If there is negativity within a person or even circling around, the best thing to do is to remove it as soon as possible. If not, once it integrates within the system, it becomes a subconscious part of that person, making it harder for a person to release and to identify without having expert help from a healer. Remember, we all want to be our true selves and maintaining goodness around us is one of the best ways.

CHAPTER 5

<u>Youth Clients</u>

The definition of youth clients for this purpose are children from ages 8-12. Because the attention span is short for the younger ones and the older ones are not yet mature to understand what is happening, you have to do a different type of Reiki healing. The kids will not always be still or quiet for 10, let alone 30 minutes. So, I allow them to talk while sending them Reiki energy remotely. With each conversation, I can probe deeper into their imagination and remove negative emotions and blockages, which removes internalized negative views. I find it beneficial when I can get a child to discuss dreams, family, and friends. From there, I can see the doors opening for the energy to move in and heal any situation. By the end of the conversation, I may even get the younger child to sit for five minutes or more to meditate, if need be. How you handle this will be unique to the youth.

One thing for sure when working with kids, trust that the energy knows this is a child and will work appropriately for the age. If you are not used to working with children, especially youth who may have emotional or physical issues, it is best for you to refrain until you take a few classes or trainings on how to work with them. Try to practice on children who are family or friends of the family to help you understand the personality traits. It takes a lot of patience and focus to keep the channel of energy open with a child who may suffer from serious emotional, mental, or physical trauma. Most abused children cannot clearly express their feelings and thoughts, so you must speak their language or at least know how to interpret it. The best scenario is a Reiki healer working with a family or child therapist to help youth heal completely.

If you have experience working with children, Reiki sessions will be a beneficial time for you as you help youth refocus, heal, and get back on their life path. I believe that if children had sessions with Reiki healers in the same manner as their regular check-ups with medical professionals, there would be happier adults in this world who understand how to work through challenging life situations without hurting others.

CHAPTER 6

<u>Animal Clients</u>

If you want to work with animals, it is good to learn about the internal organ and energy system of each. Animals are highly sensitive to energy. It is important to know when to stop. There are times when an animal will only need three minutes of Reiki. This is still just as effective as 30 minutes for the animal.

As a dog owner, I am familiar with their internal makeup. Pre-Reiki, I helped to heal and ease symptoms in my and others' dogs whenever there was pain or suffering. In my experience, there is an unnatural heat that emanates in painful areas, so I used my energy to balance out the temperature and relax the animal. Now, as a Reiki Master, I sense energy flowing in the same manner to animals as to humans. There are still hot areas on the body, but the energy channeled moves it away. I also discovered that giving a healing massage to the animal sometimes makes it easier for both parties.

If you choose to add animals as your clientele, you may decide to volunteer for a while at an animal shelter, a veterinarian, a rescue organization, or on a farm. It can help you learn the characteristics of the animals you may decide to work with in the future. Additionally, it is a wonderful experience to learn temperaments and organ functions directly from animal experts. Nowadays, many people are also becoming certified in Animal Reiki. If that is a route you want to take, get the certification. But know that you do not need it to heal animals. Reiki can and is used on everything. Animals are included in that phrase.

CHAPTER 7

The Reiki Circle & Reiki Share

Holding a Reiki Circle or Reiki Share is a great way to share energy and practice. A Reiki Circle occurs when a healer leads a group of people who want to share and experience energy healing. The healer can conduct it in any way the hosting party desires. One way is for the Reiki healer to lead everyone in a visualization while sending Remote Reiki to the group and individuals. Another method is to place a person in the middle of the circle while the group directs energy at the person. With this method, the Reiki healer holds space and sends energy to the group. Holding space means visualizing a protective shield around the group as energy is channeled. A third way is for the Reiki healer to walk around the circle and send energy to each person through the chakras. How you host your Reiki Circle is your choice. Let your spirit guide you.

This is also an opportunity to teach people who don't know anything about Reiki but are curious. It shows them how it helps to heal and to connect to the higher self. For the record, the same experiences that may occur in an individual session will occur in a Reiki circle. If in the healing process you know who needs to open or close a chakra, or breathe, tell them. Be prepared to discuss what is experienced after the Reiki Circle. I would keep quiet on any personal messages that come to you and save those for private discussions with the person. Also, it is okay if you cannot identify which message is for whom, whatever you can mention, do it. The right person will understand the message.

A Reiki Share occurs when a group of energy healers gather and send each other healing energy. There usually is a discussion before, during, or after the Reiki Share. This helps hone skills by learning new techniques and sharing new information with each other.

Reiki Circles and Reiki Shares may be held in-person and online. The choice is yours.

CHAPTER 8

<u>The Cleansing</u>

I have found it best to let clients know in advance what to expect during and after a Reiki session. Let your client know it is best to cleanse the body internally 24-48 hours prior to a session. Tell them to eat fruits, vegetables, maybe fish, if possible. Clients should not drink alcohol or use recreational drugs during the 24–48 hours timeframe. Tell them to drink lots of water and meditate on what they want to achieve. These procedures also apply for you, the healer.

Whether the session is individual, a group, a training, or a circle, let people know the following experiences may occur:

1. Body gets cold, hot, or both

2. A cool wind may circle around the body

3. A tingling sensation on parts of the body

4. Sharp or numbing pain in parts of the body as blockages are being cleared

5. Slight or severe headache that lasts a few hours

6. Ringing in the ears, slight or intense

7. Smelling flowers or other scents

8. Intermittently crying or other feelings coming to the surface

9. Sense of lightness, as if someone had removed something

10. Being relaxed or sleepy, almost fatigued

11. Receiving messages from spirit or angelic guides

12. Visual impairment (eyes open underwater, unable to see clearly)

13. Pain in eyes, blurry vision, calcium deposits releasing

14. Seeing colors, bright light, or orbs of light

15. Sudden shouting as a release

16. Experiencing a rush of energy moving throughout the body

17. Increase or start of prophetic dreams

18. Ability to remember dreams

19. Remembering past lives

20. A temporal shift sensation

21. Hearing an inner voice to guide in times of need

22. Continuous feelings of peace, happiness, contentment

23. Release of anger, hostility, resentment

24. Increase of love, understanding, acceptance

25. Release of all fear and loneliness

26. Feelings of being loved by God and the Universe

27. Strong connection to others

CHAPTER 9

<u>Visualizations</u>

Many people are using manifesting to realize a goal or achieve a specific purpose in their life. Through visualizing the outcome, they believe that the goal can come into existence. I believe in using guided visualizations in my practice. As discussed, they are meaningful for clients when guided spiritually. Not that the ones used and taught in certification classes are not beneficial, but my spirit prefers to give unique meditations for certain situations and people. Once a person relaxes in the healing process, be it in a Reiki session or in a meditation, assisting by guided visualization will enhance the result if performed properly.

As we know, people are brilliant at hiding things that are embarrassing, humiliating, painful, or worse, inhumane. They believe the incident is locked away and that it will not affect their everyday life. But that isn't true. As energy healers, we can sense the type of energy and, at the higher levels, even the entities, surrounding the body because of the denial.

We know and understand how challenging life experiences can alter a person's energy and physical health, causing attachments and blockages throughout the body. The integration of guided visualizations with Reiki also helps those persons who are having trouble focusing and releasing. I have had clients request I give them visualizations to calm them or to keep them from dozing into sleep during a session. Though, a healing sleep is not a problem as long as that is what the body requires. Either way, if there is something that is hidden, a visualization will bring it up to the conscious mind so a discussion and resolution may take place afterwards.

Everyone can use the healing visualizations in this handbook for professional and private practice. A Reiki or energy healer using the meditations and affirmations will send healing energy to the person or group. Whereas the non-healer meditating will use the visualizations to go inward to speak with the higher self for self-healing and understanding. Reiki healer or not, I hope you find them to be beneficial in your life.

CHAPTER 10

<u>The Chakras</u>

I have already mentioned the use of chakras with energy healing. Chakras are energy portals within and above the body. Having a knowledge of the chakra system increased my healing knowledge and ability. The use of the symbols I learned became clear once I knew the chakra system. The knowledge made it easier to understand the energy bodies of my clients, making me a more effective healer. Also, when a client feels a release from a particular area, I can let my client know what it represents so they will know what to focus on in their life meditations. Discussing chakras with clients also helps to stimulate memory recovery in session.

If you are unfamiliar with chakras, it is fine. It will not stop you from performing a good healing session as long as you follow your teachings. For those who want to know a little more, a brief description of the seven main chakras and a few minor ones I typically use within my practice are listed below.

The seven main chakras:

Root chakra–Located in the pelvic area at the base of the spine, helps you become grounded and handles your sense of security and stability.

Sacral chakra–Located below your belly button, represents your sexual and creative energy and how you relate to your emotions and the emotions of others.

Solar Plexus chakra–Located in your stomach area, represents confidence, self-esteem, and belief of how much control you have in your life.

Heart chakra–Located near your heart in the center of the chest, is all about our ability to love and show compassion to others and ourselves.

Throat chakra–Located in your throat, represents the ability to communicate in a clear manner.

Third eye chakra–Located between your eyes, handles intuition and foresight.

Crown chakra–Located at the top of your head, represents your spiritual connection to yourself, others, and the Universe.

The minor chakras (not inclusive):

Bindu chakra–Located near the top of the back of the head, this represents pure consciousness that exists beyond time, space, energy, matter, or form. It is a gateway to our life force.

Ear chakras–Located next to and somewhat above each ear, this represents powers of clairaudience, communication, and divine connection. It handles our ability to hear in the spiritual realm and to hear deeper truths words spoken in this realm of existence.

Hand chakras–Located in the center of the hand, the palm can send and receive energy and is the focal point for meridians and energy points throughout the body. It can also stimulate other chakras within the body.

Knee chakras–Located in the back of the knees, these work in partnership with the root chakra and represent stabilization and grounding. We also know them as a bridge between the spirit world and the physical world.

Feet chakras–Located at the bottom of the feet, these are recognized for grounding and detoxifying the body as negative energy moves from the energy centers down to the feet and out into the Earth. They connect us to Earth and its energetic field to maintain balance.

CHAPTER 11

<u>Self-Practice</u>

Before reading the chapters listing guided meditations and affirmations, I want to give you two personal affirmations to meditate on for at least 15 minutes each. Be sure you are in a quiet place, relax, and take three deep breaths with your eyes closed. Set a timer if needed and write any impressions you receive once completed. These affirmations are meant to help guide you as you help guide others.

I welcome you on this amazing journey into spirit and healing.

Affirmation 1:

"Those who react in the flesh shall never see the spirit."

Affirmation 2:

"Trust your true self, for spirit never lies to the house that keeps it safe."

CHAPTER 12

Guided Meditations

As with all healing sessions and meditations, eyes may be opened or closed. You may spiritually alter any of the visualizations listed below but try them out as written first.

Meditation 1–Chakra Cleansing

Step 1: Set your intentions. Take three cleansing breaths, cleansing breaths remove stagnant air in the body, breathe in through the nose, out through the mouth using the stomach not the chest. Try to inhale for five seconds and exhale for five seconds. Take your time. Throughout this meditation, breathe deeply using the stomach only. If you need to take a cleansing breath, do so. I may also tell you to take one if needed. Also, make sure you remain relaxed throughout the meditation. If your body tenses, take a cleansing breath and loosen up.

Now, let's open your chakras. Focus on each chakra and visualize a circle, door, or a flower opening. If you don't sense it, it's okay, you will. Also, if something else comes to mind, that is fine. Let your spirit guide you.

(While leading though the main seven chakras opening, be sure to let clients know it is okay to go at their own pace. Space out each opening as the energy tells you. You may also continue opening up secondary chakras such as, the back of the head, ears, palms, knees, feet, and anywhere else should the spirit tells you to instruct. This takes 10 minutes to complete. Pause between each chakra to allow each person to visualize and sense the chakras opening.)

Step 2: We will start with the root chakra in the pelvis area, picture a circle opening, a door opening, or the petals of a flower opening. As you open each one, if you sense there is something inside that should not be there, allow the energy to move through that chakra and lift it out, back into the Universe where it belongs. Let's go to the sacral chakra above the root, below the navel, open. Move up to the solar plexus, above the navel, below the rib cage, open. Go up to the heart chakra, in the center of the chest, open. Continue up to the throat chakra in the center, open. Now go up to the third eye in the center of the forehead, open. Finally, the crown chakra at the top of the head, open.

(Once the final chakra is open, wait 5-10 minutes for the energy to move within each chakra and energy points.)

Step 3: Now, I want you to think of an incident, situation, person, or idea that brings negative emotions and sense where it is in a chakra. It can be located in an open chakra or any another place on the body. Whatever your first thought is the correct one. Allow that negative situation, person, or idea to form in that chakra. Take your time. Once it has formed, see how it began and ended, recognize your role, accept it, and allow the energy to move it back into the Universe from where it came. Take your time and take a cleansing breath. Once it has moved out, imagine that area being sealed by light, a healing light.

(Wait at least 5-10 minutes before repeating this instruction.)

Now, if finished with that chakra, think of another situation, person, or idea and do the same. Remember, take your time. There is no need to rush. Move at your own pace.

(Do this for at least three of the major chakras, all seven if time allows, before moving to the next instruction.)

Let's close all our chakras.

(Guide the closing of the chakras starting at the crown down to the root. If secondary chakras were open go back

up to the one closest to the crown to close those also, i.e., back of the head, ears, hands, knees, feet.)

I want you to take three cleansing breaths. Allow the energy to guide you back to the present, back to awareness. Once you are ready, open your eyes, take your time moving, stretch, if needed, and let's discuss.

(Discussion is optional and depends on the type of session taking place.)

Meditation 2–Chakra Cleansing (Flower Naming)

Step 1: Set your intentions. Take three cleansing breaths, cleansing breaths remove stagnant air in the body, breathe in through the nose, out through the mouth using the stomach not the chest. Try to inhale for five seconds and exhale for five seconds. Take your time. Throughout this meditation, breathe deeply using the stomach only. If you believe you need to take a cleansing breath, do so. I may also tell you to take one if it is required. Also, make sure you remain relaxed throughout the meditation. If your body tenses, take a cleansing breath and loosen up.

Now, let's open your chakras.

(While leading though the chakras opening, be sure to let clients know it is okay to go at their own pace. Space out each opening as the energy tells you. You may also continue with opening up secondary chakras such as, the back of the head, ears, palms, knees, feet, and anywhere else should the spirit tells you to instruct. This takes 10 minutes to complete as you will pause between each chakra to allow each person to visualize and sense the chakras opening.)

Step 2: We will start with the root chakra in the pelvis area, picture a circle opening, a door opening, or the petals of a flower opening. As you open each one, if you

sense there is something inside that should not be there, allow the energy to move through that chakra and lift it back into the Universe where it belongs. Let's go to the sacral chakra above the root, below the navel, open. Move up to the solar plexus, above the navel, below the rib cage, open. Go up to the heart chakra, in the center of the chest, open. Continue up to the throat chakra in the center, open. Now go up to the third eye in the center of the forehead, open. Finally, the crown chakra at the top of the head, open.

(Once the final chakra is open, wait 5-10 minutes for the energy to move within each chakra and energy points.)

Step 3: Imagine a beautiful cloudless day. You are standing in a field of flowers. the grass tickles your feet as it comes between your toes. You walk through a small dirt path, feeling the vibration of Earth. The sun is high in the sky, shining a warm, healing light upon your skin. The sweet aroma of flowers surrounds you. Your spirit tells you that this is a special field, one in which you may leave anything that does not serve or benefit your higher purpose in life.

Alternative Step 3: Think of a person who has hurt or angered you. This person may have violated your trust, used you, or took something important away from you. It may be multiple persons. Name them, even if more than one name, and pick the same number of flowers for each name. Place each flower in a chakra, let your spirit guide you. See the flower disappear within as it cleanses away that name.

(Wait 5-10 minutes before next instruction.)

Alternative Step 3: Now think of an incident that caused you pain or sadness. Remember how it occurred, the role you played in it, how it ended, how you wanted it to end. Give a name and pick a flower for each that comes to mind. Place the flower in a chakra, allowing your spirit to guide you. See the flower disappear as it cleanses.

(Wait 5-10 minutes and repeat instructions using the terms situation and idea. Remember, to remind the person more than one situation or idea may be applied.)

Let's close all our chakras.

(Guide the closing of the chakras starting at the crown down to the root. If secondary chakras are open, go back up to the one closest to the crown to close those also, i.e., back of the head, ears, hands, knees, feet.)

I want you to take three cleansing breaths and breathe deeply as the energy guides you back to the present time, back to awareness. Once you are ready, open your eyes, take your time moving, stretch, if needed, and let's discuss.

(Discussion is optional and depends on the type of session taking place.)

Meditation 3–Grounding (water)

Step 1: Set your intentions. Take three cleansing breaths, cleansing breaths remove stagnant air in the body, breathe in through the nose, out through the mouth using the stomach not the chest. Try to inhale for five seconds and exhale for five seconds. Take your time. Throughout this meditation, breathe deeply using the stomach only. If you sense the need to take a cleansing breath, do so. I may also tell you to take one if it is required. Also, make sure you remain relaxed throughout the meditation. If your body tenses, take a cleansing breath and relax.

Now, let's open your chakras.

(While leading though the chakras opening, be sure to let clients know it is okay to go at their own pace. Space out each opening as the energy tells you. You may also continue with opening up secondary chakras such as, the back of the head, ears, palms, knees, feet, and anywhere else should the spirit tells you to instruct. This takes 10 minutes to complete as you will pause between each chakra to allow each person to visualize and sense the chakras opening.)

Step 2: We will start with the root chakra in the pelvis area, picture a circle opening, a door opening, or the petals of a flower opening. As you open each one, if you

believe there is something inside that should not be there, allow the energy to move through that chakra and lift it back into the Universe where it belongs. Let's go to the sacral chakra above the root, below the navel, open. Move up to the solar plexus, above the navel, below the rib cage, open. Go up to the heart chakra, in the center of the chest, open. Continue up to the throat chakra in the center, open. Now go up to the third eye in the center of the forehead, open. Finally, the crown chakra at the top of the head, open.

Step 3: You are standing barefoot on the shore watching the waves flow towards you. Tiny grains move between your toes as you move your feet beneath the sand. The edge of the waters touches the tip of your feet. It is chilly on your skin. You take a few steps into the waves, up to your ankles. There is a small current running from the bottom of your feet upwards. Stay in this moment and let the energy from the water replenish you. Allow the wet sand to absorb all your troubles, worries, and negative energy. Bring all thoughts to mind that do not serve so that you may cleanse in the water. Let the energy guide you and go as far as you want into the waves.

(Continue sending reiki for the rest of the session, begin closing the chakras.)

Let's close the chakras.

(Guide the closing of the chakras starting at the crown down to the root. If secondary chakras are open, go back up to the one closest to the crown to close those also, i.e., back of the head, ears, hands, knees, feet.)

I want you to take three cleansing breaths and breathe deeply. Once you are ready, open your eyes, take your time moving, stretch, if needed, and let's discuss.

(Discussion is optional and depends on the type of session taking place.)

Meditation 4–Enhance Grounding (land)

Step 1: Set your intentions. Take three cleansing breaths, cleansing breaths remove stagnant air in the body, breathe in through the nose, out through the mouth using the stomach not the chest. Try to inhale for five seconds and exhale for five seconds. Take your time. Throughout this meditation, breathe deeply using the stomach only. If you sense the need to take a cleansing breath, do so. I may also tell you to take one if it is required. Also, make sure you remain relaxed throughout the meditation. If your body tenses, take a cleansing breath and loosen up.

Now, let's open your chakras.

(While leading though the chakras opening, be sure to let clients know it is okay to go at their own pace. Space out each opening as the energy tells you. You may also continue with opening up secondary chakras such as, the back of the head, ears, palms, knees, feet, and anywhere else should the spirit tells you to instruct. This takes 10 minutes to complete as you will pause between each chakra to allow each person to visualize and sense the chakras opening.)

Step 2: We will start with the root chakra in the pelvis area, picture a circle opening, a door opening, or the petals of a flower opening. As you open each one, if you

sense there is something inside that should not be there, allow the energy to move through that chakra and lift it back into the Universe where it belongs. Let's go to the sacral chakra above the root, below the navel, open. Move up to the solar plexus, above the navel, below the rib cage, open. Go up to the heart chakra, in the center of the chest, open. Continue up to the throat chakra in the center, open. Now go up to the third eye in the center of the forehead, open. Finally, the crown chakra at the top of the head, open.

Step 3: Imagine laying on the earth in an open field. The grass is soft beneath your body. The sun is shining down upon your skin. You are merging with the earth as the warmth of the sun pores into your chakras. Bring forth all thoughts of goodness and happiness to each chakra. Allow the earth to absorb all emotions that do not serve you as the light from the sun cleanses you. Let your spirit and the energy guide you on this journey as you become one with the planet.

(Continue sending reiki for the rest of the session, begin closing the chakras.)

Let's close the chakras.

(Guide the closing of the chakras starting at the crown down to the root. If secondary chakras are open, go back

up to the one closest to the crown to close those also, i.e., back of the head, ears, hands, knees, feet.)

I want you to take three cleansing breaths and breathe deeply. Once you are ready, open your eyes, take your time moving, stretch, if needed, and let's discuss.

(Discussion is optional and depends on the type of session taking place.)

Meditation 5–Releasing Negative Incidents

Step 1: Set your intentions. Take three cleansing breaths, cleansing breaths remove stagnant air in the body, breathe in through the nose, out through the mouth using the stomach not the chest. Try to inhale for five seconds and exhale for five seconds. Take your time. Throughout this meditation, breathe deeply using the stomach only. If you sense the need to take a cleansing breath, do so. I may also tell you to take one. Also, make sure you remain relaxed throughout the meditation. If your body is tensing, take a cleansing breath and loosen up.

Now, let's open your chakras.

(While leading though the chakras opening, be sure to let clients know it is okay to go at their own pace. Space out each opening as the energy tells you. You may also continue with opening up secondary chakras such as, the back of the head, ears, palms, knees, feet, and anywhere else should the spirit tells you to instruct. This takes 10 minutes to complete as you will pause between each chakra to allow each person to visualize and sense the chakras opening.)

Step 2: We will start with the root chakra in the pelvis area, picture a circle opening, a door opening, or the petals of a flower opening. As you open each one, if you

believe there is something inside that should not be there, allow the energy to move through that chakra and lift it back into the Universe where it belongs. Let's go to the sacral chakra above the root, below the navel, open. Move up to the solar plexus, above the navel, below the rib cage, open. Go up to the heart chakra, in the center of the chest, open. Continue up to the throat chakra in the center, open. Now go up to the third eye in the center of the forehead, open. Finally, the crown chakra at the top of the head, open.

(Once the final chakra is open, wait 5-10 minutes for the energy to move within each chakra and energy points.)

Step 3: Now, I want you to think of an incident that brings negative emotions and sense where it is in a chakra. It can be in a chakra opened or another part on the body. Whatever your first thought is the correct one. Allow that negative incident to form in that chakra. Take your time. Once it has formed, see how it began and ended, recognize your role, accept it. Allow the energy to move it out, back into the Universe from where it came. Take your time and take a cleansing breath. Once it has moved out, imagine that area being sealed by a healing light. Allow the energy to move freely.

(Repeat at least two to four more times. You may point out periods in the life, such as youth, adulthood, work, or

school. Wait 5-10 minutes before moving to the next instruction in between each incident.)

Let's close all our chakras.

(Guide the closing of the chakras starting at the crown down to the root. If secondary chakras are open, go back up to the one closest to the crown to close those also, i.e., back of the head, ears, hands, knees, feet.)

I want you to take three cleansing breaths and breathe deeply as the energy guides you back to the present time, back to awareness. Once you are ready, open your eyes, take your time moving, stretch, if needed, and let's discuss.

(Discussion is optional and depends on the type of session taking place.)

Meditation 6–Releasing Negative Situations

Step 1: Set your intentions. Take three cleansing breaths, cleansing breaths remove stagnant air in the body, breathe in through the nose, out through the mouth using the stomach not the chest. Try to inhale for five seconds and exhale for five seconds. Take your time. Throughout this meditation, breathe deeply using the stomach only. If you sense the need to take a cleansing breath, do so. I may also tell you to take one. Also, make sure you remain relaxed throughout the meditation. If you sense your body tensing, take a cleansing breath and loosen up.

Now, let's open your chakras.

(While leading though the chakras opening, be sure to let clients know it is okay to go at their own pace. Space out each opening as the energy tells you. You may also continue with opening up secondary chakras such as, the back of the head, ears, palms, knees, feet, and anywhere else should the spirit tells you to instruct. This takes 10 minutes to complete as you will pause between each chakra to allow each person to visualize and sense the chakras opening.)

Step 2: We will start with the root chakra in the pelvis area, picture a circle opening, a door opening, or the petals of a flower opening. As you open each one, if you

think there is something inside that should not be there, allow the energy to move through that chakra and lift it back into the Universe where it belongs. Let's go to the sacral chakra above the root, below the navel, open. Move up to the solar plexus, above the navel, below the rib cage, open. Go up to the heart chakra, in the center of the chest, open. Continue up to the throat chakra in the center, open. Now go up to the third eye in the center of the forehead, open. Finally, the crown chakra at the top of the head, open.

(Once the final chakra is open, wait 5-10 minutes for the energy to move within each chakra and energy points.)

Step 3: Now, I want you to think of a situation that brings negative emotions and notice where it is in a chakra. It can be in a chakra we opened or another chakra on the body. Whatever your first thought is the correct one. Allow that negative situation to form in that chakra. Take your time. Once it has formed, see how it began and ended, recognize your role, accept it. Allow the energy to move it out, back into the Universe from where it came. Take your time and take a cleansing breath. Once it has moved out, imagine that area being sealed a healing light.

(Repeat at least two to four more times. You may point out periods in the life, such as youth, adulthood, work,

school. Wait 5-10 minutes before moving to the next instruction in between each incident.)

Let's close all our chakras.

(Guide the closing of the chakras starting at the crown down to the root. If secondary chakras are open, go back up to the one closest to the crown to close those also, i.e., back of the head, ears, hands, knees, feet.)

I want you to take three cleansing breaths and breathe deeply as the energy guides you back to the present time, back to awareness. Once you are ready, open your eyes, take your time moving, stretch, if needed, and let's discuss.

(Discussion is optional and depends on the type of session taking place.)

Meditation 7–Releasing Effects of Negative/Difficult Persons

Step 1: Set your intentions. Take three cleansing breaths, cleansing breaths remove stagnant air in the body, breathe in through the nose, out through the mouth using the stomach not the chest. Try to inhale for five seconds and exhale for five seconds. Take your time. Throughout this meditation, breathe deeply using the stomach only. If you notice a need to take a cleansing breath, do so. I may also tell you to take one. Also, make sure you remain relaxed throughout the meditation. If your body is tensing, take a cleansing breath and loosen up.

Now, let's open up your chakras.

(While leading though the chakras opening, be sure to let clients know it is okay to go at their own pace. Space out each opening as the energy tells you. You may also continue with opening up secondary chakras such as, the back of the head, ears, palms, knees, feet, and anywhere else should the spirit tells you to instruct. This takes 10 minutes to complete as you will pause between each chakra to allow each person to visualize the chakras opening.)

Step 2: We will start with the root chakra in the pelvis area, picture a circle opening, a door opening, or the

petals of a flower opening. As you open each one, if you notice there is something inside that should not be there, allow the energy to move through that chakra and lift it back into the Universe where it belongs. Let's go to the sacral chakra above the root, below the navel, open. Move up to the solar plexus, above the navel, below the rib cage, open. Go up to the heart chakra, in the center of the chest, open. Continue up to the throat chakra in the center, open. Now go up to the third eye in the center of the forehead, open. Finally, the crown chakra at the top of the head, open.

(Once the final chakra is open, wait 5-10 minutes for the energy to move within each chakra and energy points.)

Step 3: Now, I want you to think of a person who brings negative emotions and where it is in a chakra. It can be in a chakra we opened or another chakra on the body. Whatever your first thought is the correct one. Allow that person to form in that chakra. Take your time. Once it has formed, see how it began and ended, recognize your role, accept it. Allow the energy to move it out, back into the Universe from where it came. Take your time and take a cleansing breath. Once it has moved out, imagine that area being sealed by light, a healing light.

(Repeat at least two to four more times. You may point out periods in the life, such as youth, adulthood, work,

school. Wait 5-10 minutes before moving to the next instruction in between each incident.)

Let's close all our chakras.

(Guide the closing of the chakras starting at the crown down to the root. If secondary chakras were opened, go back up to the one closest to the crown to start closing those also, i.e., back of the head, ears, hands, knees, feet.)

I want you to take three cleansing breaths and breathe deeply as the energy guides you back to the present time, back to awareness. Once you are ready, open your eyes, take your time moving, stretch, if needed, and let's discuss.

(Discussion is optional and depends on the type of session taking place.)

Meditation 8–Releasing Negative Ideas/Thoughts

Step 1: Set your intentions. Take three cleansing breaths, cleansing breaths remove stagnant air in the body, breathe in through the nose, out through the mouth using the stomach not the chest. Try to inhale for five seconds and exhale for five seconds. Take your time. Throughout this meditation, breathe deeply using the stomach only. If you notice a need to take a cleansing breath, do so. I may also tell you to take one if needed. Also, make sure you remain relaxed throughout the meditation. If your body tenses, take a cleansing breath and loosen up.

Now, let's open your chakras.

(While leading though the chakras opening, be sure to let clients know it is okay to go at their own pace. Space out each opening as the energy tells you. You may also continue with opening up secondary chakras such as, the back of the head, ears, palms, knees, feet, and anywhere else should the spirit tells you to instruct. This usually takes 10 minutes to complete as you will pause between each chakra to allow each person to visualize and sense the chakras opening.)

Step 2: We will start with the root chakra in the pelvis area, picture a circle opening, a door opening, or the petals of a flower opening. As you open each one, if you

notice there is something inside that should not be there, allow the energy to move through that chakra and lift it back into the Universe where it belongs. Let's go to the sacral chakra above the root, below the navel, open. Move up to the solar plexus, above the navel, below the rib cage, open. Go up to the heart chakra, in the center of the chest, open. Continue up to the throat chakra in the center, open. Now go up to the third eye in the center of the forehead, open. Finally, the crown chakra at the top of the head, open.

(Once the final chakra is open, wait 5-10 minutes for the energy to move within each chakra and energy points.)

Step 3: Now, I want you to think of an idea that brings negative emotions and where it is in a chakra. It can be in a chakra we opened or another chakra on the body. Whatever your first thought is the correct one. Allow that negative idea to form in that chakra. Take your time. Once it has formed, see how it began and ended, recognize your role, accept it. Allow the energy to move it out, back into the Universe from where it came. Take your time and take a cleansing breath. Once it has moved out, imagine that area being sealed by light, a healing light.

(Repeat at least two to four more times. You may point out periods in the life, such as youth, adulthood, work,

school. Wait 5-10 minutes before moving to the next instruction in between each incident.)

Let's close all our chakras.

(Guide the closing of the chakras starting at the crown down to the root. If secondary chakras are open, go back up to the one closest to the crown to close those also, i.e., back of the head, ears, hands, knees, feet.)

I want you to take three cleansing breaths and breathe deeply as the energy guides you back to the present time, back to awareness. Once you are ready, open your eyes, take your time moving, stretch, if needed, and let's discuss.

(Discussion is optional and depends on the type of session taking place.)

Meditation 9–Releasing Insecurities & Fears

Step 1: Set your intentions. Take three cleansing breaths, cleansing breaths remove stagnant air in the body, breathe in through the nose, out through the mouth using the stomach not the chest. Try to inhale for five seconds and exhale for five seconds. Take your time. Throughout this meditation, breathe deeply using the stomach only. If you sense the need to take a cleansing breath, do so. I may also tell you to take one. Also, make sure you remain relaxed throughout the meditation. If your body tenses, take a cleansing breath and loosen up.

Now, let's open your chakras.

(While leading though the chakras opening, be sure to let clients know it is okay to go at their own pace. Space out each opening as the energy tells you. You may also continue with opening up secondary chakras such as, the back of the head, ears, palms, knees, feet, and anywhere else should the spirit tells you to instruct. This usually takes 10 minutes to complete as you will pause between each chakra to allow each person to visualize and hopefully sense the chakras opening.)

Step 2: We will start with the root chakra in the pelvis area, picture a circle opening, a door opening, or the petals of a flower opening. As you open each one, if you

believe there is something inside that should not be there, allow the energy to move through that chakra and lift it back into the Universe where it belongs. Let's go to the sacral chakra above the root, below the navel, open. Move up to the solar plexus, above the navel, below the rib cage, open. Go up to the heart chakra, in the center of the chest, open. Continue up to the throat chakra in the center, open. Now go up to the third eye in the center of the forehead, open. Finally, the crown chakra at the top of the head, open.

(Once the final chakra is open, wait 5-10 minutes for the energy to move within each chakra and energy points.)

Step 3: I want you to imagine you are in an open field sitting in the grass; at the beach or lake sitting on the shore; or wherever your spirit takes you. While sitting, the sun's rays move across your body, the light is brilliant and pure. You notice an energy from the rays enter your chakras and energy points throughout your body, cleansing away the layers that do not serve your higher purpose. You sense each chakra opening wider as the energy swirls around you, creating an orb of healing.

Alternative Step 3: Now I want you to visualize your spirit rising outside your body and sitting in front of you. It is an exact duplicate of you watching as the energy moves through you. Think about something that causes you insecurity. It can be a person, situation, or incident from the past or present. Think about it and see where that emotion is on your body. It can be in a shoulder, a knee, your arm, anywhere. Once you sense it, give it a color and allow it to expand. Let the emotion take over your body until there is nothing else. Go slow.

Alternative Step 3: Allow the feelings to expand around you until it fills up an orb with colors. Once you are at the place where it is overwhelming, permit your spirit to reach over and touch the orb. Move all the negative emotion and anything attached to it back into the Universe.

Alternative Step 3: I want you to think about something-person, place, situation, etc., that makes you afraid. Do the same thing as before, sense it on your body, give it a color and let it take over until it is impossible to continue. Allow your spirit to move outside your body and touch the colored orb. Move the fear and all that is attached to it back into the Universe, with goodness and light. Take your time. Now feel you, as the spirit, stand and move towards the orb, becoming one again with the physical self. You feel content, peaceful. Take a cleansing breath, inhaling all that pure, healing energy. Sit in this moment and feel the surrounding goodness.

Let's close all our chakras.

(Guide the closing of the chakras starting at the crown down to the root. If secondary chakras are open, go back up to the one closest to the crown to close those also, i.e., back of the head, ears, hands, knees, feet.)

I want you to take three cleansing breaths and breathe deeply as the energy guides you back to the present time, back to awareness. Once you are ready, open your eyes, take your time moving, stretch, if needed, and let's discuss.

(Discussion is optional and depends on the type of session taking place.)

(You may repeat the visualization using the following emotions: doubt, jealousy, envy, hate. You may also add any other negative emotion if your spirit tells you.)

Meditation 10–Controlling Anxiety/Panic attacks

Step 1: Set your intentions. Take three cleansing breaths, cleansing breaths remove stagnant air in the body, breathe in through the nose, out through the mouth using the stomach not the chest. Try to inhale for five seconds and exhale for five seconds. Take your time. Throughout this meditation, breathe deeply using the stomach only. If you notice a need to take a cleansing breath, do so. I may also tell you to take one. Also, make sure you remain relaxed throughout the meditation. If your body tenses, take a cleansing breath and loosen up.

Now, let's open your chakras.

(While leading though the chakras opening, be sure to let clients know it is okay to go at their own pace. Space out each opening as the energy tells you. You may also continue with opening up secondary chakras such as, the back of the head, ears, palms, knees, feet, and anywhere else should the spirit tells you to instruct. This takes 10 minutes to complete as you will pause between each chakra to allow each person to visualize the chakras opening.)

Step 2: We will start with the root chakra in the pelvis area, picture a circle opening, a door opening, or the petals of a flower opening. As you open each one, if you

believe there is something inside that should not be there, allow the energy to move through that chakra and lift it back into the Universe where it belongs. Let's go to the sacral chakra above the root, below the navel, open. Move up to the solar plexus, above the navel, below the rib cage, open. Go up to the heart chakra, in the center of the chest, open. Continue up to the throat chakra in the center, open. Now go up to the third eye in the center of the forehead, open. Finally, the crown chakra at the top of the head, open.

Step 3: Remember the last situations where you had an anxiety/panic attack. See the trigger in each situation and the emotion rising inside you. Ask your spirit why is it there? How can you release it? Allow the energy to guide you as you release your body to the emotion. Do not hold back, allow it to overcome and overwhelm. Let your spirit take over. Watch your spirit remove it and replace it with peace.

(Continue sending reiki for the rest of the session, begin closing the chakras.)

Let's close the chakras.

(Guide the closing of the chakras starting at the crown down to the root. If secondary chakras are open, go back

up to the one closest to the crown to close those also, i.e., back of the head, ears, hands, knees, feet.)

I want you to take three cleansing breaths and breathe deeply. Once you are ready, open your eyes, take your time moving, stretch, if needed, and let's discuss.

(Discussion is optional and depends on the type of session taking place.)

Meditation 11–Releasing Negative Energy (Spirit Walk)

Step 1: Set your intentions. Take three cleansing breaths, cleansing breaths remove stagnant air in the body, breathe in through the nose, out through the mouth using the stomach not the chest. Try to inhale for five seconds and exhale for five seconds. Take your time. Throughout this meditation, breathe deeply using the stomach only. If you notice the need to take a cleansing breath, do so. I may also tell you to take one if needed. Also, make sure you remain relaxed throughout the meditation. If your body tenses, take a cleansing breath and loosen up.

Now, let's open your chakras.

(While leading though the chakras opening, be sure to let clients know it is okay to go at their own pace. Space out each opening as the energy tells you. You may also continue with opening up secondary chakras such as, the back of the head, ears, palms, knees, feet, and anywhere else should the spirit tells you to instruct. This usually takes 10 minutes to complete as you will pause between each chakra to allow each person to visualize and sense the chakras opening.)

Step 2: We will start with the root chakra in the pelvis area, picture a circle opening, a door opening, or the petals of a flower opening. As you open each one, if you

notice there is something inside that should not be there, allow the energy to move through that chakra and lift it up back into the Universe where it belongs. Let's go to the sacral chakra above the root, below the navel, open. Move up to the solar plexus, above the navel, below the rib cage, open. Go up to the heart chakra, in the center of the chest, open. Continue up to the throat chakra in the center, open. Now go up to the third eye in the center of the forehead, open. Finally, the crown chakra at the top of the head, open.

(Once the final chakra is open, wait 5-10 minutes for the energy to move within each chakra and energy points.)

Step 3: Imagine that you are walking in a place of your choosing. Take in the scenery. Notice the colors, the smells, the sounds, and if there are people or animals, see them walking around as well. As you are walking notice a subtle change in your surroundings. The air becomes thick as you inhale and you notice there are things or people, maybe both, that bring about negative emotions in you. Take a cleansing breath.

Now, walk towards the thing that causes that negative emotion, whether it is anger, sadness, fear, anxiety, stress. Walk in that direction and focus your sight. What is it made of? What color appears to you? How did it end up in your life?

Let your spirit and the energy guide you, and remove it from your presence, back into the Universe. Take your time.

(Wait 10-15 minutes before next instruction. During the process, continue to encourage the client to look deeper, be honest, to be strong... Remind the person about the healing energy cleansing away the negative emotions/blockages and to take cleansing breaths as needed.)

If you're ready, do the same with any person who comes upon your walk. Who is that person? Why do you not like them? Why does their presence cause such negative emotions? Remember, let your spirit and healing energy guide you. Allow the energy to show you, to teach you, and to heal you. As each thing or person disappears, you are lighter, more at peace.

(Wait 10-15 minutes before next instruction.)

Let's close all our chakras.

(Guide the closing of the chakras starting at the crown down to the root. If secondary chakras are open, go back up to the one closest to the crown to close those also, i.e., back of the head, ears, hands, knees, feet.)

I want you to take three cleansing breaths and breathe deeply as the energy guides you back to the present time, back to awareness. Once you are ready, open your eyes, take your time moving, stretch, if needed, and let's discuss.

(Discussion is optional and depends on the type of session taking place.)

Meditation 12–Healing from Breakups

Step 1: Set your intentions. Take three cleansing breaths, cleansing breaths remove stagnant air in the body, breathe in through the nose, out through the mouth using the stomach not the chest. Try to inhale for five seconds and exhale for five seconds. Take your time. Throughout this meditation, breathe deeply using the stomach only. If you sense the need to take a cleansing breath, do so. I may also tell you to take one. Also, make sure you remain relaxed throughout the meditation. If your body is tensing, take a cleansing breath and loosen up.

Now, let's open your chakras.

(While leading though the chakras opening, be sure to let clients know it is okay to go at their own pace. Space out each opening as the energy tells you. You may also continue with opening up secondary chakras such as, the back of the head, ears, palms, knees, feet, and anywhere else should the spirit tells you to instruct. This takes 10 minutes to complete as you will pause between each chakra to allow each person to visualize and sense the chakras opening.)

Step 2: We will start with the root chakra in the pelvis area, picture a circle opening, a door opening, or the petals of a flower opening. As you open each one, if you

notice there is something inside that should not be there, allow the energy to move through that chakra and lift it back into the Universe where it belongs. Let's go to the sacral chakra above the root, below the navel, open. Move up to the solar plexus, above the navel, below the rib cage, open. Go up to the heart chakra, in the center of the chest, open. Continue up to the throat chakra in the center, open. Now go up to the third eye in the center of the forehead, open. Finally, the crown chakra at the top of the head, open.

Step 3: Picture the person who you believe broke your heart. Visualize all the good things that person did for you, all the things you liked about the person. Allow those feelings to go into all your chakras, to permeate your being.

(Wait about 10-15 minutes.)

Now think about the things you did not like, the things that hurt you and move all of it to your third eye chakra. Repeat this statement in your mind, "That person was an addition to my life, not my life's mission." Continue repeating this in your mind while you move the negative emotions to the third eye chakra.

(Continue sending reiki for the rest of the session, begin closing the chakras.)

Let's close the chakras.

(Guide the closing of the chakras starting at the crown down to the root. If secondary chakras are open, go back up to the one closest to the crown to close those also, i.e., back of the head, ears, hands, knees, feet.)

I want you to take three cleansing breaths and breathe deeply. Once you are ready, open your eyes, take your time moving, stretch, if needed, and let's discuss.

(Discussion is optional and depends on the type of session taking place.)

Meditation 13–Connecting with your Spirit Body

Step 1: Set your intentions. Take three cleansing breaths, cleansing breaths remove stagnant air in the body, breathe in through the nose, out through the mouth using the stomach not the chest. Try to inhale for five seconds and exhale for five seconds. Take your time. Throughout this meditation, breathe deeply using the stomach only. If you need to take a cleansing breath, do so. I may also tell you to take one if needed. Also, make sure you remain relaxed throughout the meditation. If your body tenses, take a cleansing breath and loosen up.

Now, let's open your chakras.

(While leading though the chakras opening, be sure to let clients know it is okay to go at their own pace. Space out each opening as the energy tells you. You may also continue with opening up secondary chakras such as, the back of the head, ears, palms, knees, feet, and anywhere else should the spirit tells you to instruct. This takes 10 minutes to complete as you will pause between each chakra to allow each person to visualize and notice the chakras opening.)

Step 2: We will start with the root chakra in the pelvis area, picture a circle opening, a door opening, or the petals of a flower opening. As you open each one, if you

believe there is something inside that should not be there, allow the energy to move through that chakra and lift it back into the Universe where it belongs. Let's go to the sacral chakra above the root, below the navel, open. Move up to the solar plexus, above the navel, below the rib cage, open. Go up to the heart chakra, in the center of the chest, open. Continue up to the throat chakra in the center, open. Now go up to the third eye in the center of the forehead, open. Finally, the crown chakra at the top of the head, open.

(Once the final chakra is open, wait 5-10 minutes for the energy to move within each chakra and energy points.)

Step 3: I want you to visualize your spirit outside your body. See it as a perfect copy of you. Now as the energy is moving through each chakra, see it connect the chakras of your physical body with that of the spiritual body outside you. Take your time and allow the connection, the oneness.

(Wait 5-10 minutes before the next instruction.)

Now see as your spirit body reaches out and begins pulling negative energy from each connected chakra. As the negative energy comes out, name it. Whatever the first name you think of is correct. Don't hesitate. Remain open and honest. And as you name it, anything attached to that name that is from your past, present, and even future, allow your spirit to pull those blockages from that chakra. Send them back to the Universe and out of your physical body. Go slow, take your time for each chakra until there is none left for your spirit to clean.

(Wait 15-20 minutes before next instruction. During this time, you may request cleansing breaths as the energy builds or to release emotions. You may remind that it can be any time period. Remind clients to be honest, not to fear, and any other instruction you receive from the energy while you allow the meditation to complete.)

Now allow your spirit body to move back inside your frame. Permit it become one with you, notice the healing energy and light emanating from within. Allow that light to circle around you, creating an orb of healing energy. See it focus in on anything left in your chakras that do not serve your higher purpose, like grains of sand, and allow it to filter those grains out of the orb. Do not hold it.

(Wait 5-10 minutes before next instruction.)

Let's close all our chakras.

(Guide the closing of the chakras starting at the crown down to the root. If secondary chakras are open, go back up to the one closest to the crown to close those also, i.e., back of the head, ears, hands, knees, feet.)

I want you to take three cleansing breaths and breathe deeply as the energy guides you back to the present time, back to awareness. Once you are ready, open your eyes, take your time moving, stretch, if needed, and let's discuss.

(Discussion is optional and depends on the type of session taking place.)

Meditation 14–Connecting with your Spirit (Talk)

Step 1: Set your intentions. Take three cleansing breaths, cleansing breaths remove stagnant air in the body, breathe in through the nose, out through the mouth using the stomach not the chest. Try to inhale for five seconds and exhale for five seconds. Take your time. Throughout this meditation, breathe deeply using the stomach only. If you need to take a cleansing breath, do so. I may also tell you to take one if needed. Also, make sure you remain relaxed throughout the meditation. If you become tense, take a cleansing breath and loosen up.

Now, let's open your chakras.

(While leading though the chakras opening, be sure to let clients know it is okay to go at their own pace. Space out each opening as the energy tells you. You may also continue with opening up secondary chakras such as, the back of the head, ears, palms, knees, feet, and anywhere else should the spirit tells you to instruct. This takes 10 minutes to complete as you will pause between each chakra to allow each person to visualize and notice the chakras opening.)

Step 2: We will start with the root chakra in the pelvis area, picture a circle opening, a door opening, or the petals of a flower opening. As you open each one, if you

believe there is something inside that should not be there, allow the energy to move through that chakra and lift back into the Universe where it belongs. Let's go to the sacral chakra above the root, below the navel, open. Move up to the solar plexus, above the navel, below the rib cage, open. Go up to the heart chakra, in the center of the chest, open. Continue up to the throat chakra in the center, open. Now go up to the third eye in the center of the forehead, open. Finally, the crown chakra at the top of the head, open.

(Once the final chakra is open, wait 5-10 minutes for the energy to move within each chakra and energy points.)

Step 3: I want you to imagine that you are sitting in a room full of light. The energy emanates around you, entering all your chakras. There is a sense of calmness and peace swirling around you. Take a moment to enjoy this emotion, this cleansing, as your chakras and energetic channels open wider.

(Wait 5-10 minutes before next instruction.)

Now sense another presence in the room, and visualize a form take shape in front of you. As the figure becomes more solid, you realize it's your spirit. You take the hands of your spirit as a conversation begins between you both. The spirit tells you about all the attached pain, fear, and worry as you listen, waiting. Allow the energy to guide you in response, to help you remove those emotions that do not serve you, to bring calmness to your body.

(Wait 15-20 minutes before next instruction.)

Once the conversation is complete, hug your spirit, bringing it back within your body. Accept the togetherness, the wholeness of both. Acknowledge the energy emanating from inside you, moving through your body to your aura and energy body, making you complete.

(Wait 5-10 minutes before next instruction.)

Let's close all our chakras.

(Guide the closing of the chakras starting at the crown down to the root. If secondary chakras are open, go back up to the one closest to the crown to close those also, i.e., back of the head, ears, hands, knees, feet.)

I want you to take three cleansing breaths and breathe deeply as the energy guides you back to the present time, back to awareness. Once you are ready, open your eyes, take your time moving, stretch, if needed, and let's discuss.

(Discussion is optional and depends on the type of session taking place.)

Meditation 15–Connecting with Energy

Step 1: Set your intentions. Take three cleansing breaths, cleansing breaths remove stagnant air in the body, breathe in through the nose, out through the mouth using the stomach not the chest. Try to inhale for five seconds and exhale for five seconds. Take your time. Throughout this meditation, breathe deeply using the stomach only. If you need to take a cleansing breath, do so. I may also tell you to take one. Also, make sure you remain relaxed throughout the meditation. If you tense, take a cleansing breath and loosen up.

Now, let's open your chakras.

(While leading though the chakras opening, be sure to let clients know it is okay to go at their own pace. Space out each opening as the energy tells you. You may also continue with opening up secondary chakras such as, the back of the head, ears, palms, knees, feet, and anywhere else should the spirit tells you to instruct. This takes 10 minutes to complete as you will pause between each chakra to allow each person to visualize and notice the chakras opening.)

Step 2: We will start with the root chakra in the pelvis area, picture a circle opening, a door opening, or the petals of a flower opening. As you open each one, if you

believe there is something inside that should not be there, allow the energy to move through that chakra and lift it back into the Universe where it belongs. Let's go to the sacral chakra above the root, below the navel, open. Move up to the solar plexus, above the navel, below the rib cage, open. Go up to the heart chakra, in the center of the chest, open. Continue up to the throat chakra in the center, open. Now go up to the third eye in the center of the forehead, open. Finally, the crown chakra at the top of the head, open.

Step 3: Right now, in the space, I want you to relax your body; let the energy move around you. Allow your mind to see the various colors that move towards your third eye. Sense the vibration of each as they move inside. Allow access to good energy as it removes all darkness back into the universe from which it came. Let the energy encompass you, focus on nothing else but emotion and letting go. Release all control.

(Continue sending reiki for the rest of the session, begin closing the chakras.)

Let's close the chakras.

(Guide the closing of the chakras starting at the crown down to the root. If secondary chakras are open, go back

up to the one closest to the crown to close those also, i.e., back of the head, ears, hands, knees, feet.)

I want you to take three cleansing breaths and breathe. Once you are ready, open your eyes, take your time moving, stretch, if needed, and let's discuss.

(Discussion is optional and depends on the type of session taking place.)

Meditation 16–Finding your True Self

Step 1: Set your intentions. Take three cleansing breaths, cleansing breaths remove stagnant air in the body, breathe in through the nose, out through the mouth using the stomach not the chest. Try to inhale for five seconds and exhale for five seconds. Take your time. Throughout this meditation, breathe deeply using the stomach only. If you sense the need to take a cleansing breath, do so. I may also tell you to take one. Also, make sure you remain relaxed throughout the meditation. If you sense your body tensing, take a cleansing breath and loosen up.

Now, let's open your chakras.

(While leading though the chakras opening, be sure to let clients know it is okay to go at their own pace. Space out each opening as the energy tells you. You may also continue with opening up secondary chakras such as, the back of the head, ears, palms, knees, feet, and anywhere else should the spirit tells you to instruct. This takes 10 minutes to complete as you will pause between each chakra to allow each person to visualize and sense the chakras opening.)

Step 2: We will start with the root chakra in the pelvis area, picture a circle opening, a door opening, or the petals of a flower opening. As you open each one, if you

notice there is something inside that should not be there, allow the energy to move through that chakra and lift it back into the Universe where it belongs. Let's go to the sacral chakra above the root, below the navel, open. Move up to the solar plexus, above the navel, below the rib cage, open. Go up to the heart chakra, in the center of the chest, open. Continue up to the throat chakra in the center, open. Now go up to the third eye in the center of the forehead, open. Finally, the crown chakra at the top of the head, open.

(Once the final chakra is open, wait 5-10 minutes for the energy to move within each chakra and energy points.)

Step 3: Visualize this room with you laying on the table. Experience the separateness of you with the surroundings, the hardness of the table, the temperature of the room, the sounds in the air. Hear your breathing and notice how your body moves as you inhale and exhale.

(Wait a few minutes, 5-10, as your client adjusts to the visualization.)

Start focusing inward, on every organ, muscle, tissue, bone, and flesh.

(Wait 5-10 minutes again.)

Go deeper with each cell moving in your body, flowing through every part. Now, see what does not belong within, that which is not a part of you, let it move out into the aura, back into the universe. Allow your true self awakening, see it rising from slumber.

(Continue giving reiki as your client moves into a deep healing state. Be cognizant of the changes in the body and atmosphere and allow the energy to flow to those areas needing healing. This is also a perfect time to cleanse the aura and send reiki to the person's spiritual body.)

Let's close all our chakras.

(Guide the closing of the chakras starting at the crown down to the root. If secondary chakras are open, go back up to the one closest to the crown to close those also, i.e., back of the head, ears, hands, knees, feet.)

I want you to take three cleansing breaths and breathe deeply as the energy guides you back to the present time, back to awareness. Once you are ready, open your eyes, take your time moving, stretch, if needed, and let's discuss.

(Discussion is optional and depends on the type of session taking place.)

Meditation 17–Finding the Authentic You

Step 1: Set your intentions. Take three cleansing breaths, cleansing breaths remove stagnant air in the body, breathe in through the nose, out through the mouth using the stomach not the chest. Try to inhale for five seconds and exhale for five seconds. Take your time. Throughout this meditation, breathe deeply using the stomach only. If you need to take a cleansing breath, do so. I may also tell you to take one. Also, make sure you remain relaxed throughout the meditation. If your body tenses, take a cleansing breath and loosen up.

Now, let's open your chakras.

(While leading though the chakras opening, be sure to let clients know it is okay to go at their own pace. Space out each opening as the energy tells you. You may also continue with opening up secondary chakras such as, the back of the head, ears, palms, knees, feet, and anywhere else should the spirit tells you to instruct. This takes 10 minutes to complete as you will pause between each chakra to allow each person to visualize and sense the chakras opening.)

Step 2: We will start with the root chakra in the pelvis area, picture a circle opening, a door opening, or the petals of a flower opening. As you open each one, if you

believe there is something inside that should not be there, allow the energy to move through that chakra and lift it back into the Universe where it belongs. Let's go to the sacral chakra above the root, below the navel, open. Move up to the solar plexus, above the navel, below the rib cage, open. Go up to the heart chakra, in the center of the chest, open. Continue up to the throat chakra in the center, open. Now go up to the third eye in the center of the forehead, open. Finally, the crown chakra at the top of the head, open.

Step 3: Allow your mind to go to a situation where you did or said something you did not want. See the face you are wearing; notice every detail. Imagine it lifting as you say or do what you want. Continue thinking of these situations and lifting away the mask. See your true face each time, the real you, the authentic you. Let the energy guide you.

(Continue sending reiki for the rest of the session, begin closing the chakras.)

Let's close the chakras.

(Guide the closing of the chakras starting at the crown down to the root. If secondary chakras are open, go back up to the one closest to the crown to close those also, i.e., back of the head, ears, hands, knees, feet.)

I want you to take three cleansing breaths and breathe deeply. Once you are ready, open your eyes, take your time moving, stretch, if needed, and let's discuss.

(Discussion is optional and depends on the type of session taking place.)

Meditation 18–Acknowledging your Shadow Self

Step 1: Set your intentions. Take three cleansing breaths, cleansing breaths remove stagnant air in the body, breathe in through the nose, out through the mouth using the stomach not the chest. Try to inhale for five seconds and exhale for five seconds. Take your time. Throughout this meditation, breathe deeply using the stomach only. If you need to take a cleansing breath, do so. I may also tell you to take one. Also, make sure you remain relaxed throughout the meditation. If your body tenses, take a cleansing breath and loosen up.

Now, let's open your chakras.

(While leading though the chakras opening, be sure to let clients know it is okay to go at their own pace. Space out each opening as the energy tells you. You may also continue with opening up secondary chakras such as, the back of the head, ears, palms, knees, feet, and anywhere else should the spirit tells you to instruct. This takes 10 minutes to complete as you will pause between each chakra to allow each person to visualize and sense the chakras opening.)

Step 2: We will start with the root chakra in the pelvis area, picture a circle opening, a door opening, or the petals of a flower opening. As you open each one, if you

notice there is something inside that should not be there, allow the energy to move through that chakra and lift back into the Universe where it belongs. Let's go to the sacral chakra above the root, below the navel, open. Move up to the solar plexus, above the navel, below the rib cage, open. Go up to the heart chakra, in the center of the chest, open. Continue up to the throat chakra in the center, open. Now go up to the third eye in the center of the forehead, open. Finally, the crown chakra at the top of the head, open.

Step 3: As the energy moves through your body, I want you to focus on an experience in which you wronged another person or something you dislike about your personality. Let it play over in your mind and think of other situations where you exhibited similar behavior. Be honest with yourself. This is between you, your spirit, and the universe.

(Wait 10-15 minutes before continuing.)

Think about the emotion or characteristic you put forth to the other person. Now locate where it is on your body. Imagine it being absorbed up into a beaming light.

(Wait about 5-10 minutes before continuing.)

Now, see those persons you hurt being healed and cleansed as you release that darkness inside you.

(Wait about 5-10 minutes before continuing.)

Let's close the chakras.

(Guide the closing of the chakras starting at the crown down to the root. If secondary chakras are open, go back up to the one closest to the crown to close those also, i.e., back of the head, ears, hands, knees, feet.)

I want you to take three cleansing breaths and breathe deeply. Once you are ready, open your eyes, take your time moving, stretch, if needed, and let's discuss.

(Discussion is optional and depends on the type of session taking place.)

Meditation 19–Discovering your Past Lives

Step 1: Set your intentions. Take three cleansing breaths, cleansing breaths remove stagnant air in the body, breathe in through the nose, out through the mouth using the stomach not the chest. Try to inhale for five seconds and exhale for five seconds. Take your time. Throughout this meditation, breathe deeply using the stomach only. If you need to take a cleansing breath, do so. I may also tell you to take one. Also, make sure you remain relaxed throughout the meditation. If you feel your body tensing, take a cleansing breath and loosen up.

Step 2: We will start with the root chakra in the pelvis area, picture a circle opening, a door opening, or the petals of a flower opening. As you open each one, if you believe there is something inside that should not be there, allow the energy to move through that chakra and lift it back into the Universe where it belongs. Let's go to the sacral chakra above the root, below the navel, open. Move up to the solar plexus, above the navel, below the rib cage, open. Go up to the heart chakra, in the center of the chest, open. Continue up to the throat chakra in the center, open. Now go up to the third eye in the center of the forehead, open. Finally, the crown chakra at the top of the head, open.

Step 3: Let's go to another place and time. Picture yourself living many lifetimes ago. Release everything from this world, your face, your body, your family, your friends. This world no longer exists. Now see who you used to be. See your family and friends in that time.

(Wait about 10 minutes for the client to adjust, ask the next questions or whichever questions your spirit requests of you. Wait at least 3 minutes in between each question before preceding to the next.)

Who are you?

What are you doing?

What struggles do you have?

How is your life?

How did you die?

What is your character?

(Continue to send reiki to those areas where your spirit guides you. Once you are towards the end of the session, about 10 minutes, go to Step 4.)

Step 4: Remember the emotions and feelings you have in that life. Bring them back to this present life. Notice the similarities. What did you bring from that life into this one?

(Wait about 10 minutes before moving to the next step.)

Let's close all our chakras.

(Guide the closing of the chakras starting at the crown down to the root. If secondary chakras are open, go back up to the one closest to the crown to close those also, i.e., back of the head, ears, hands, knees, feet.)

I want you to take three cleansing breaths and breathe deeply. Once you are ready, open your eyes, take your time moving, stretch, if needed, and let's discuss.

(Discussion is optional and depends on the type of session taking place.)

Meditation 20–Reconnecting with Past Life (animal)

Step 1: Set your intentions. Take three cleansing breaths, cleansing breaths remove stagnant air in the body, breathe in through the nose, out through the mouth using the stomach not the chest. Try to inhale for five seconds and exhale for five seconds. Take your time. Throughout this meditation, breathe deeply using the stomach only. If you discover the need to take a cleansing breath, do so. I may also tell you to take one. Also, make sure you remain relaxed throughout the meditation. If your body tenses, take a cleansing breath and loosen up.

Now, let's open your chakras.

(While leading though the chakras opening, be sure to let clients know it is okay to go at their own pace. Space out each opening as the energy tells you. You may also continue with opening up secondary chakras such as, the back of the head, ears, palms, knees, feet, and anywhere else should the spirit tells you to instruct. This takes 10 minutes to complete as you will pause between each chakra to allow each person to visualize and sense the chakras opening.)

Step 2: We will start with the root chakra in the pelvis area, picture a circle opening, a door opening, or the petals of a flower opening. As you open each one, if there

is something inside that should not be there, allow the energy to move through that chakra and lift it back into the Universe where it belongs. Let's go to the sacral chakra above the root, below the navel, open. Move up to the solar plexus, above the navel, below the rib cage, open. Go up to the heart chakra, in the center of the chest, open. Continue up to the throat chakra in the center, open. Now go up to the third eye in the center of the forehead, open. Finally, the crown chakra at the top of the head, open.

Step 3: Remove yourself from this time, from this body. See the other life when you were yet human. See your animal self. Notice the surroundings and your life there. Let the energy show you what you were and how you came to be here right now. Release control and allow the energy and your spirit self to guide you.

(Continue sending reiki for the rest of the session, begin closing the chakras.)

Let's close the chakras.

(Guide the closing of the chakras starting at the crown down to the root. If secondary chakras are open, go back up to the one closest to the crown to close those also, i.e., back of the head, ears, hands, knees, feet.)

I want you to take three cleansing breaths and breathe deeply. Once you are ready, open your eyes, take your time moving, stretch, if needed, and let's discuss.

(Discussion is optional and depends on the type of session taking place.)

Meditation 21–Healing your Aura

Step 1: Set your intentions. Take three cleansing breaths, cleansing breaths remove stagnant air in the body, breathe in through the nose, out through the mouth using the stomach not the chest. Try to inhale for five seconds and exhale for five seconds. Take your time. Throughout this meditation, breathe deeply using the stomach only. If there is a need to take a cleansing breath, do so. I may also tell you to take one. Also, make sure you remain relaxed throughout the meditation. If you your body tenses, take a cleansing breath.

Now, let's open your chakras.

(While leading though the chakras opening, be sure to let clients know it is okay to go at their own pace. Space out each opening as the energy tells you. You may also continue with opening up secondary chakras such as, the back of the head, ears, palms, knees, feet, and anywhere else should the spirit tells you to instruct. This takes 10 minutes to complete as you will pause between each chakra to allow each person to visualize and sense the chakras opening.)

Step 2: We will start with the root chakra in the pelvis area, picture a circle opening, a door opening, or the petals of a flower opening. As you open each one, there

is something inside that should not be there, allow the energy to move through that chakra and lift it back into the Universe where it belongs. Let's go to the sacral chakra above the root, below the navel, open. Move up to the solar plexus, above the navel, below the rib cage, open. Go up to the heart chakra, in the center of the chest, open. Continue up to the throat chakra in the center, open. Now go up to the third eye in the center of the forehead, open. Finally, the crown chakra at the top of the head, open.

Step 3: See yourself sitting under an enormous tree in the center of an open field. The grass and flowers are swaying back and forth with the breeze. You hear the sounds of nature as you look upwards in the sky, the cool breeze touches your skin. As the wind circles around, you see a ray of white light moving towards you. This is a healing light from the universe moving to your crown chakra, creating a white orb around you, filling up your aura. As the energy moves around you, sense the parts within your aura that don't belong. Whether it is a person, emotion, belief, let it form, see it move back into the blue sky, out of your aura, back into the universe.

(Continue sending reiki for the rest of the session, begin closing the chakras.)

Let's close the chakras.

(Guide the closing of the chakras starting at the crown down to the root. If secondary chakras are open, go back up to the one closest to the crown to close those also, i.e., back of the head, ears, hands, knees, feet.)

I want you to take three cleansing breaths and breathe deeply. Once you are ready, open your eyes, take your time moving, stretch, if needed, and let's discuss.

(Discussion is optional and depends on the type of session taking place.)

Meditation 22–Releasing Childhood Trauma

Step 1: Set your intentions. Take three cleansing breaths, cleansing breaths remove stagnant air in the body, breathe in through the nose, out through the mouth using the stomach not the chest. Try to inhale for five seconds and exhale for five seconds. Take your time. Throughout this meditation, breathe deeply using the stomach only. If there is a need to take a cleansing breath, do so. I may also tell you to take one. Also, make sure you remain relaxed throughout the meditation. If your body tenses, take a cleansing breath and loosen up.

Now, let's open your chakras.

(While leading though the chakras opening, be sure to let clients know it is okay to go at their own pace. Space out each opening as the energy tells you. You may also continue with opening up secondary chakras such as, the back of the head, ears, palms, knees, feet, and anywhere else should the spirit tells you to instruct. This takes 10 minutes to complete as you will pause between each chakra to allow each person to visualize the chakras opening.)

Step 2: We will start with the root chakra in the pelvis area, picture a circle opening, a door opening, or the petals of a flower opening. As you open each one, there

is something inside that should not be there, allow the energy to move through that chakra and lift it back into the Universe where it belongs. Let's go to the sacral chakra above the root, below the navel, open. Move up to the solar plexus, above the navel, below the rib cage, open. Go up to the heart chakra, in the center of the chest, open. Continue up to the throat chakra in the center, open. Now go up to the third eye in the center of the forehead, open. Finally, the crown chakra at the top of the head, open.

(Once the final chakra is open, wait 5-10 minutes for the energy to move within each chakra and energy points.)

Step 3: I want you to imagine that you are sitting in a room full of light. The energy emanates around you, entering all your chakras. There is a sense of calmness and peace swirling around you. Take a moment to enjoy this cleansing, as your chakras and energetic channels open wider.

(Wait 5-10 minutes before next instruction.)

Now sense another presence in the room. A small form take shape in front of you. As the figure becomes more solid, you realize it's you as a child. You take the hands of the child as a conversation begins between you both. The child tells you about all the experienced pain, fear, and worry as you listen, waiting. Allow your spirit to guide you in response, to help you remove those fears, to bring calmness to the child.

(Wait 15-20 minutes before next instruction.)

Once the conversation is complete, hug the child, bringing the child back within your body. Enjoy the togetherness the wholeness of both. See how the child has affected you the adult and release any attachments back into the Universe from that child.

(Wait 5-10 minutes before next instruction.)

Let's close all our chakras.

(Guide the closing of the chakras starting at the crown down to the root. If secondary chakras are open, go back up to the one closest to the crown to close those also, i.e., back of the head, ears, hands, knees, feet.)

I want you to take three cleansing breaths and breathe deeply as the energy guides you back to the present time, back to awareness. Once you are ready, open your eyes, take your time moving, stretch, if needed, and let's discuss.

(Discussion is optional and depends on the type of session taking place.)

Meditation 23–Releasing Childhood Trauma (Specific Issue)

Step 1: Set your intentions. Take three cleansing breaths, cleansing breaths remove stagnant air in the body, breathe in through the nose, out through the mouth using the stomach not the chest. Try to inhale for five seconds and exhale for five seconds. Take your time. Throughout this meditation, breathe deeply using the stomach only. If there is the need to take a cleansing breath, do so. I may also tell you to take one. Also, make sure you remain relaxed throughout the meditation. If your body is tensing, take a cleansing breath and loosen up.

Now, let's open your chakras.

(While leading though the chakras opening, be sure to let clients know it is okay to go at their own pace. Space out each opening as the energy tells you. You may also continue with opening up secondary chakras such as, the back of the head, ears, palms, knees, feet, and anywhere else should the spirit tells you to instruct. This takes 10 minutes to complete as you will pause between each chakra to allow each person to visualize the chakras opening.)

Step 2: We will start with the root chakra in the pelvis area, picture a circle opening, a door opening, or the

petals of a flower opening. As you open each one, if there is something inside that should not be there, allow the energy to move through that chakra and lift it back into the Universe where it belongs. Let's go to the sacral chakra above the root, below the navel, open. Move up to the solar plexus, above the navel, below the rib cage, open. Go up to the heart chakra, in the center of the chest, open. Continue up to the throat chakra in the center, open. Now go up to the third eye in the center of the forehead, open. Finally, the crown chakra at the top of the head, open.

(Once the final chakra is open, wait 5-10 minutes for the energy to move within each chakra and energy points. Move into the meditation and name the specific issue needing to be released.)

Step 3: Now let's go back to the root chakra. Imagine a moment in your childhood when you experienced hurt/fear/anger, etc.... Visualize the scenery, the location, the people present. Hear the words spoken by them, by you. Let the feelings resurface, take them out of the hiding place in the root chakra and allow yourself to experience everything. Remain honest, don't run away. Watch everything and allow the emotions to move away from your body back into the universe. Allow the energy to take all that away.

(You may continue this for the length of the session focusing on the removal of multiple traumas within one area or work on several chakras for the length of the session.)

Let's close all our chakras.

(Guide the closing of the chakras starting at the crown down to the root. If secondary chakras are open, go back up to the one closest to the crown to close those also, i.e., back of the head, ears, hands, knees, feet.)

I want you to take three cleansing breaths and breathe deeply as the energy guides you back to the present time, back to awareness. Once you are ready, open your eyes, take your time moving, stretch, if needed, and let's discuss.

(Discussion is optional and depends on the type of session taking place.)

Meditation 24–Releasing Trauma from Sexual or Physical Abuse

Step 1: Set your intentions. Take three cleansing breaths, cleansing breaths remove stagnant air in the body, breathe in through the nose, out through the mouth using the stomach not the chest. Try to inhale for five seconds and exhale for five seconds. Take your time. Throughout this meditation, breathe deeply using the stomach only. If you need to take a cleansing breath, do so. I may also tell you to take one if needed. Also, make sure you remain relaxed throughout the meditation. If your body tenses, take a cleansing breath and loosen up.

Now, let's open your chakras.

(While leading though the chakras opening, be sure to let clients know it is okay to go at their own pace. Space out each opening as the energy tells you. You may also continue with opening up secondary chakras such as, the back of the head, ears, palms, knees, feet, and anywhere else should the spirit tell you to instruct. This takes 5-10 minutes to complete as you will pause between each chakra to allow each person to visualize the chakras opening.)

Step 2: We will start with the root chakra in the pelvis area, picture a circle opening, a door opening, or the

petals of a flower opening. As you open each one, if you believe there is something inside that should not be there, allow the energy to move through that chakra and lift it back into the Universe where it belongs. Let's go to the sacral chakra above the root, below the navel, open. Move up to the solar plexus, above the navel, below the rib cage, open. Go up to the heart chakra, in the center of the chest, open. Continue up to the throat chakra in the center, open. Now go up to the third eye in the center of the forehead, open. Finally, the crown chakra at the top of the head, open.

(Once the final chakra is open, wait 5-10 minutes for the energy to move within each chakra and energy points.)

Step 3: Take three cleansing breaths, cleansing breaths remove stagnant air in the body, breathe in through the nose, out through the mouth using the stomach not the chest. Try to inhale for five seconds and exhale for five seconds. Take your time. Throughout this meditation, breathe deeply using the stomach only. If there is a need to take a cleansing breath, do so. I may also tell you to take one if needed. Also, make sure you remain relaxed throughout the meditation. If you believe your body is tensing, take a cleansing breath and loosen up.

Step 4: Remember you are in a safe space; nothing here can harm you. Pretend you are watching a movie and you are the main character. Play the incident in your mind. Keep everything in your third eye and crown chakra. If you have any emotions moving within your heart or any other chakra, do not close it. Visualize it moving upwards to the third eye and crown, back up into the universe. Let the energy remove all blockages and release everything that does not serve the higher purpose.

(Keep reminding the person who they are in a safe space and focus on allowing the energy to flow through you to those areas most in need of healing. Be cognizant of the emotions that may arise and if needed stop the session for prior discussion or silent meditation with the client. You may still send Reiki while meditating with your client. Be sure to follow procedure and close all the chakras before the client leaves.)

Let's close all our chakras.

(Guide the closing of the chakras starting at the crown down to the root. If secondary chakras are open, go back up to the one closest to the crown to close those also, i.e., back of the head, ears, hands, knees, feet.)

Meditation 25–Internal Healing

Step 1: Set your intentions. Take three cleansing breaths, cleansing breaths remove stagnant air in the body, breathe in through the nose, out through the mouth using the stomach not the chest. Try to inhale for five seconds and exhale for five seconds. Take your time. Throughout this meditation, breathe deeply using the stomach only. If you need to take a cleansing breath, do so. I may also tell you to take one if needed. Also, make sure you remain relaxed throughout the meditation. If you believe your body is tensing, take a cleansing breath and loosen up.

Now, let's open your chakras.

(While leading though the chakras opening, be sure to let clients know it is okay to go at their own pace. Space out each opening as the energy tells you. You may also continue with opening up secondary chakras such as, the back of the head, ears, palms, knees, feet, and anywhere else should the spirit tells you to instruct. This takes 10 minutes to complete as you will pause between each chakra to allow each person to visualize the chakras opening.)

Step 2: We will start with the root chakra in the pelvis area, picture a circle opening, a door opening, or the petals of a flower opening. As you open each one, if there

is something inside that should not be there, allow the energy to move through that chakra and lift back into the Universe where it belongs. Let's go to the sacral chakra above the root, below the navel, open. Move up to the solar plexus, above the navel, below the rib cage, open. Go up to the heart chakra, in the center of the chest, open. Continue up to the throat chakra in the center, open. Now go up to the third eye in the center of the forehead, open. Finally, the crown chakra at the top of the head, open.

Step 3: I want you to imagine the inside of your body. See the areas that are not healthy. The areas not functioning. Now spiritually see them. Notice the areas where there is not light, and there is weak vibration. Allow the energy to move into the space and remove the darkness, replacing it with healing energy and cosmic vibrations. See the pain, don't experience it, watch it being lifted upwards, back into the universe.

(Continue sending reiki for the rest of the session, begin closing the chakras.)

Let's close the chakras.

(Guide the closing of the chakras starting at the crown down to the root. If secondary chakras are open, go back up to the one closest to the crown to close those also, i.e., back of the head, ears, hands, knees, feet.)

I want you to take three cleansing breaths and breathe deeply. Once you are ready, open your eyes, take your time moving, stretch, if needed, and let's discuss.

(Discussion is optional and depends on the type of session taking place.)

Meditation 26–Physical Healing

Step 1: Set your intentions. Take three cleansing breaths, cleansing breaths remove stagnant air in the body, breathe in through the nose, out through the mouth using the stomach not the chest. Try to inhale for five seconds and exhale for five seconds. Take your time. Throughout this meditation, breathe deeply using the stomach only. If you need to take a cleansing breath, do so. I may also tell you to take one if needed. Also, make sure you remain relaxed throughout the meditation. If your body tenses, take a cleansing breath and loosen up.

Now, let's open your chakras.

(While leading though the chakras opening, be sure to let clients know it is okay to go at their own pace. Space out each opening as the energy tells you. You may also continue with opening up secondary chakras such as, the back of the head, ears, palms, knees, feet, and anywhere else should the spirit tell you to instruct. This takes 10 minutes to complete as you will pause between each chakra to allow each person to visualize the chakras opening.)

Step 2: We will start with the root chakra in the pelvis area, picture a circle opening, a door opening, or the petals of a flower opening. As you open each one, if there

is something inside that should not be there, allow the energy to move through that chakra and lift it back into the Universe where it belongs. Let's go to the sacral chakra above the root, below the navel, open. Move up to the solar plexus, above the navel, below the rib cage, open. Go up to the heart chakra, in the center of the chest, open. Continue up to the throat chakra in the center, open. Now go up to the third eye in the center of the forehead, open. Finally, the crown chakra at the top of the head, open.

Step 3: Let the pain take over your entire body. Focus in on nothing else. Once it is to where you cannot take it anymore, imagine it being siphoned into an orb of light. See the orb get bigger as the pain moves within. Let your body relax, fully accept, integrate what it left into every cell and see them unfolding back to the original state. Keep going until the pain decreases, or it becomes tolerable.

(Continue sending reiki for the rest of the session, begin closing the chakras.)

Let's close the chakras.

(Guide the closing of the chakras starting at the crown down to the root. If secondary chakras are open, go back

up to the one closest to the crown to close those also, i.e., back of the head, ears, hands, knees, feet.)

I want you to take three cleansing breaths and breathe deeply. Once you are ready, open your eyes, take your time moving, stretch, if needed, and let's discuss.

(Discussion is optional and depends on the type of session taking place.)

Meditation 27–Accepting Death

Step 1: Set your intentions. Take three cleansing breaths, cleansing breaths remove stagnant air in the body, breathe in through the nose, out through the mouth using the stomach not the chest. Try to inhale for five seconds and exhale for five seconds. Take your time. Throughout this meditation, breathe deeply using the stomach only. If you believe the need to take a cleansing breath, do so. I may also tell you to take one. Also, make sure you remain relaxed throughout the meditation. If your body is tensing, take a cleansing breath and loosen up.

Now, let's open your chakras.

(While leading though the chakras opening, be sure to let clients know it is okay to go at their own pace. Space out each opening as the energy tells you. You may also continue with opening up secondary chakras such as, the back of the head, ears, palms, knees, feet, and anywhere else should the spirit tells you to instruct. This takes 10 minutes to complete as you will pause between each chakra to allow each person to visualize the chakras opening.)

Step 2: We will start with the root chakra in the pelvis area, picture a circle opening, a door opening, or the petals of a flower opening. As you open each one, if you

think there is something inside that should not be there, allow the energy to move through that chakra and lift it back into the Universe where it belongs. Let's go to the sacral chakra above the root, below the navel, open. Move up to the solar plexus, above the navel, below the rib cage, open. Go up to the heart chakra, in the center of the chest, open. Continue up to the throat chakra in the center, open. Now go up to the third eye in the center of the forehead, open. Finally, the crown chakra at the top of the head, open.

Step 3: You are at the top of a cliff overlooking the ocean. The calming waters make small waves beneath you, the sun is reflecting off the water causing silver white lines to come toward you. The lines move closer and closer until you notice they are moving upwards in the air, coming towards you. A cool breeze circles around you as your body moves closer to the edge. A white light rises in front of you and lifts you up into the air. You float over the ocean, taking in the scenery. You see family and friends waving at you from small islands within the water. Allow the energy to take you higher upwards, notice the lightness and sense all fear of what's coming lift away. See the new life with happiness, peace, serenity, and gratitude. Release the old life with thankfulness. Let go to start anew.

(Continue sending reiki for the rest of the session, begin closing the chakras.)

Let's close the chakras.

(Guide the closing of the chakras starting at the crown down to the root. If secondary chakras are open, go back up to the one closest to the crown to close those also, i.e., back of the head, ears, hands, knees, feet.)

I want you to take three cleansing breaths and breathe deeply. Once you are ready, open your eyes, take your time moving, stretch, if needed, and let's discuss.

(Discussion is optional and depends on the type of session taking place.)

Meditation 28–Manifesting Goals

Step 1: Set your intentions. Take three cleansing breaths, cleansing breaths remove stagnant air in the body, breathe in through the nose, out through the mouth using the stomach not the chest. Try to inhale for five seconds and exhale for five seconds. Take your time. Throughout this meditation, breathe deeply using the stomach only. If there is a need to take a cleansing breath, do so. I may also tell you to take one if needed. Also, make sure you remain relaxed throughout the meditation. If your body tenses, take a cleansing breath and loosen up.

Now, let's open your chakras.

(While leading though the chakras opening, be sure to let clients know it is okay to go at their own pace. Space out each opening as the energy tells you. You may also continue with opening up secondary chakras such as, the back of the head, ears, palms, knees, feet, and anywhere else should the spirit tell you to instruct. This takes 10 minutes to complete as you will pause between each chakra to allow each person to visualize the chakras opening.)

Step 2: We will start with the root chakra in the pelvis area, picture a circle opening, a door opening, or the petals of a flower opening. As you open each one, if there

is something inside that should not be there, allow the energy to move through that chakra and lift it back into the Universe where it belongs. Let's go to the sacral chakra above the root, below the navel, open. Move up to the solar plexus, above the navel, below the rib cage, open. Go up to the heart chakra, in the center of the chest, open. Continue up to the throat chakra in the center, open. Now go up to the third eye in the center of the forehead, open. Finally, the crown chakra at the top of the head, open.

(Be sure to discuss the particular goal so that you will know how to lead in the visualization. State the goal and the effect it will have on the person. If this is a group session or reiki circle, keep it general as written below.)

Step 3: I want you to see the outcome of your goal. It doesn't matter what it is. Vividly see it in your mind. Make it so vivid it is as if it is occurring right now. See the surrounding people, what they are wearing, what you are wearing, their faces, etc. Now go back in time to the beginning when it was an idea. Allow your spirit to guide you through the process to the outcome. Don't fight any thoughts that come to you, don't push away any visions. Be receptive to the path to the outcome. Let the reality seep in from your spirit to your physical body. Believe it is real, allow it to enter the door to your life.

(Continue sending reiki for the rest of the session, begin closing the chakras.)

Let's close the chakras.

(Guide the closing of the chakras starting at the crown down to the root. If secondary chakras are open, go back up to the one closest to the crown to close those also, i.e., back of the head, ears, hands, knees, feet.)

I want you to take three cleansing breaths and breathe deeply. Once you are ready, open your eyes, take your time moving, stretch, if needed, and let's discuss.

(Discussion is optional and depends on the type of session taking place.)

Meditation 29–Improving Communication

Step 1: Set your intentions. Take three cleansing breaths, cleansing breaths remove stagnant air in the body, breathe in through the nose, out through the mouth using the stomach not the chest. Try to inhale for five seconds and exhale for five seconds. Take your time. Throughout this meditation, breathe deeply using the stomach only. If there is a need to take a cleansing breath, do so. I may also tell you to take one if needed. Also, make sure you remain relaxed throughout the meditation. If your body tenses, take a cleansing breath and loosen up.

Now, let's open your chakras.

(While leading though the chakras opening, be sure to let clients know it is okay to go at their own pace. Space out each opening as the energy tells you. You may also continue with opening up secondary chakras such as, the back of the head, ears, palms, knees, feet, and anywhere else should the spirit tells you to instruct. This takes 10 minutes to complete as you will pause between each chakra to allow each person to visualize the chakras opening.)

Step 2: We will start with the root chakra in the pelvis area, picture a circle opening, a door opening, or the petals of a flower opening. As you open each one, if you

think there is something inside that should not be there, allow the energy to move through that chakra and lift back into the Universe where it belongs. Let's go to the sacral chakra above the root, below the navel, open. Move up to the solar plexus, above the navel, below the rib cage, open. Go up to the heart chakra, in the center of the chest, open. Continue up to the throat chakra in the center, open. Now go up to the third eye in the center of the forehead, open. Finally, the crown chakra at the top of the head, open.

Step 3: Imagine there are small balls of energy in the throat and ear chakras. Allow these balls of energy to flow within the throat, mouth and ears to clear away the blockages while picturing yourself speaking to a group of people. What emotion comes to mind? Hang on to that emotion and allow the energy to guide you to its origin, to the time created. If any other emotions come up, do the same with each.

(Continue sending reiki for the rest of the session, begin closing the chakras. Note that this can be performed when the person has difficulty communicating in any situation, such as, business, personal, or casual. Alter the visualization to suit the situation required.)

Let's close the chakras.

(Guide the closing of the chakras starting at the crown down to the root. If secondary chakras are open, go back up to the one closest to the crown to close those also, i.e., back of the head, ears, hands, knees, feet.)

I want you to take three cleansing breaths and breathe deeply. Once you are ready, open your eyes, take your time moving, stretch, if needed, and let's discuss.

(Discussion is optional and depends on the type of session taking place.)

Meditation 30–Giving Gratitude

Step 1: Set your intentions. Take three cleansing breaths, cleansing breaths remove stagnant air in the body, breathe in through the nose, out through the mouth using the stomach not the chest. Try to inhale for five seconds and exhale for five seconds. Take your time. Throughout this meditation, breathe deeply using the stomach only. If there is a need to take a cleansing breath, do so. I may also tell you to take one. Also, make sure you remain relaxed throughout the meditation. If your body is tensing, take a cleansing breath and loosen up.

Step 2: Now, let's open your chakras. As you open up each chakra, I want you to think of one thing that you are thankful for from your childhood. Insert it into each chakra with an acknowledgment of why you are thankful/grateful. We will start with the root chakra in the pelvis area. Let's go to the sacral chakra above the root, below the navel, open. Move up to the solar plexus, above the navel, below the rib cage, open. Go up to the heart chakra, in the center of the chest, open. Continue up to the throat chakra in the center, open. Now go up to the third eye in the center of the forehead, open. Finally, the crown chakra at the top of the head, open.

(Wait about 5 minutes in between each chakra for the person to visualize the one thing they are

thankful/grateful for from childhood. You may continue by having the person do the same for teen years, adult years, and future years, which is like manifesting. Continue sending reiki for the rest of the session, begin closing the chakras.)

Let's close the chakras.

(Guide the closing of the chakras starting at the crown down to the root. If secondary chakras are open, go back up to the one closest to the crown to close those also, i.e., back of the head, ears, hands, knees, feet.)

I want you to take three cleansing breaths and breathe deeply. Once you are ready, open your eyes, take your time moving, stretch, if needed, and let's discuss.

(Discussion is optional and depends on the type of session taking place.)

Meditation 31–Interpreting Dreams

Step 1: Set your intentions. Take three cleansing breaths, cleansing breaths remove stagnant air in the body, breathe in through the nose, out through the mouth using the stomach not the chest. Try to inhale for five seconds and exhale for five seconds. Take your time. Throughout this meditation, breathe deeply using the stomach only. If there is the need to take a cleansing breath, do so. I may also tell you to take one. Also, make sure you remain relaxed throughout the meditation. If your body is tensing, take a cleansing breath and loosen up.

Now, let's open your chakras.

(While leading though the chakras opening, be sure to let clients know it is okay to go at their own pace. Space out each opening as the energy tells you. You may also continue with opening up secondary chakras such as, the back of the head, ears, palms, knees, feet, and anywhere else should the spirit tell you to instruct. This takes 10 minutes to complete as you will pause between each chakra to allow each person to visualize the chakras opening.)

Step 2: We will start with the root chakra in the pelvis area, picture a circle opening, a door opening, or the petals of a flower opening. As you open each one, if you

think there is something inside that should not be there, allow the energy to move through that chakra and lift it back into the Universe where it belongs. Let's go to the sacral chakra above the root, below the navel, open. Move up to the solar plexus, above the navel, below the rib cage, open. Go up to the heart chakra, in the center of the chest, open. Continue up to the throat chakra in the center, open. Now go up to the third eye in the center of the forehead, open. Finally, the crown chakra at the top of the head, open.

Step 3: Replay the dream in your mind. We ask the energy, your spirit, to show you the meaning, to open the doors to the higher planes. Keep replaying the dream as each truth comes forth.

(Continue sending reiki for the rest of the session, begin closing the chakras.)

Let's close the chakras.

(Guide the closing of the chakras starting at the crown down to the root. If secondary chakras are open, go back up to the one closest to the crown to close those also, i.e., back of the head, ears, hands, knees, feet.)

I want you to take three cleansing breaths and breathe deeply. Once you are ready, open your eyes, take your time moving, stretch, if needed, and let's discuss.

LaTanya L. Hill, JD, Reiki Master

(Discussion is optional and depends on the type of session taking place.)

Meditation 32–Building your Spiritual House

Step 1: Set your intentions. Take three cleansing breaths, cleansing breaths remove stagnant air in the body, breathe in through the nose, out through the mouth using the stomach not the chest. Try to inhale for five seconds and exhale for five seconds. Take your time. Throughout this meditation, breathe deeply using the stomach only. If you need to take a cleansing breath, do so. I may also tell you to take one. Also, make sure you remain relaxed throughout the meditation. If your body is tensing, take a cleansing breath and loosen up.

Now, let's open up your chakras.

(While leading though the chakras opening, be sure to let clients know it is okay to go at their own pace. Space out each opening as the energy tells you. You may also continue with opening up secondary chakras such as, the back of the head, ears, palms, knees, feet, and anywhere else should the spirit tells you to instruct. This takes 10 minutes to complete as you will pause between each chakra to allow each person to visualize the chakras opening.)

Step 2: We will start with the root chakra in the pelvis area, picture a circle opening, a door opening, or the petals of a flower opening. As you open each one, if you

believe there is something inside that should not be there, allow the energy to move through that chakra and lift it back into the Universe where it belongs. Let's go to the sacral chakra above the root, below the navel, open. Move up to the solar plexus, above the navel, below the rib cage, open. Go up to the heart chakra, in the center of the chest, open. Continue up to the throat chakra in the center, open. Now go up to the third eye in the center of the forehead, open. Finally, the crown chakra at the top of the head, open.

Step 3: See yourself rising upwards into the sky, space, and into the spiritual realm. Let your spirit show you to your home, your spiritual house. Allow it to reveal areas where it needs to be fixed and areas that are perfectly sound.

(Continue sending reiki for the rest of the session, begin closing the chakras.)

Let's close the chakras.

(Guide the closing of the chakras starting at the crown down to the root. If secondary chakras are open, go back up to the one closest to the crown to close those also, i.e., back of the head, ears, hands, knees, feet.)

I want you to take three cleansing breaths and breathe deeply. Once you are ready, open your eyes, take your time moving, stretch, if needed, and let's discuss.

(Discussion is optional and depends on the type of session taking place.)

Meditation 33–Connecting with Ancestors

Step 1: Set your intentions. Take three cleansing breaths, cleansing breaths remove stagnant air in the body, breathe in through the nose, out through the mouth using the stomach not the chest. Try to inhale for five seconds and exhale for five seconds. Take your time. Throughout this meditation, breathe deeply using the stomach only. If you need to take a cleansing breath, do so. I may also tell you to take one. Also, make sure you remain relaxed throughout the meditation. If your body is tensing, take a cleansing breath and loosen up.

Now, let's open your chakras.

(While leading though the chakras opening, be sure to let clients know it is okay to go at their own pace. Space out each opening as the energy tells you. You may also continue with opening up secondary chakras such as, the back of the head, ears, palms, knees, feet, and anywhere else should the spirit tells you to instruct. This takes 10 minutes to complete as you will pause between each chakra to allow each person to visualize the chakras opening.)

Step 2: We will start with the root chakra in the pelvis area, picture a circle opening, a door opening, or the petals of a flower opening. As you open each one, if you

believe there is something inside that should not be there, allow the energy to move through that chakra and lift it back into the Universe where it belongs. Let's go to the sacral chakra above the root, below the navel, open. Move up to the solar plexus, above the navel, below the rib cage, open. Go up to the heart chakra, in the center of the chest, open. Continue up to the throat chakra in the center, open. Now go up to the third eye in the center of the forehead, open. Finally, the crown chakra at the top of the head, open.

Step 3: See your spirit lifting out of your body. Watch as it goes into the spiritual realm. There are many people around. Visualize who comes forth to speak with you and hear the message given. Keep your crown and third eye chakra open wide to receive all ancestors of good willing to come forth.

(Continue sending reiki for the rest of the session, begin closing the chakras.)

Let's close the chakras.

(Guide the closing of the chakras starting at the crown down to the root. If secondary chakras are open, go back up to the one closest to the crown to close those also, i.e., back of the head, ears, hands, knees, feet.)

I want you to take three cleansing breaths and breathe deeply. Once you are ready, open your eyes, take your time moving, stretch, if needed, and let's discuss.

(Discussion is optional and depends on the type of session taking place.)

CHAPTER 13

Affirmations

Use these for daily or weekly meditations. Try to repeat for at least 15 minutes and build up to 60 minutes or more. You may change the phrasing to suit yourself but try them as written first.

1. I connect to the Universe, to God energy, and to my spirit so I may return to the Oneness.

2. As I walk in the natural, may the Universe guide my path and open all doors of goodness.

3. My words are power and binding; I speak with clarity, perfection, and truth.

4. I hear what is silent, what is hidden, what is spoken.

5. I open my heart to the Universe as it sends divine love within me.

6. I am who my spirit wants me to be, I remove society's imprint.

7. I am a creation of and within the Universe, goodness surrounds me.

8. I am energy - separate and same. I inhale as you exhale.

9. I remove all illusions placed upon me and clear all visions before me; I am here.

10. Fear is a spirit attached to my being, may the Universe release and receive it with love.

11. This house is a temporary vessel; I give it no importance over the spirit living inside.

12. I ask God energy to clear my path so I may walk with perfection and peace.

13. May energy of good enter my chakras to clear all that does not serve my higher purpose.

14. I release my spirit from all contracts and agreements that do not fulfill complete elements of goodness and light.

15. I am a being of light within flesh, may all who see me be illuminated by good.

16. Negative words and perceptions cannot touch me for I am bathed in God energy, pure goodness, and light.

17. I refute all negativity projected upon me for I walk in truth, goodness, and light.

18. I am the Universe, and the Universe is me, we shall not be separated by fleshly desires.

19. I forgive those who have hurt me as they are a part of me, and the pain inflicted is a reflection of their own.

20. I remove the mask that was created for me and seek my true face as my spirit awakens.

21. I request a clearing of all debts from this life and previous lives so that my spirit may be unbound and free.

22. I ask my Angels of Good to surround and protect me from anything that would do me harm, intentionally or spiritually.

23. I extend my circle of protection to my family and friends, may the energy of goodness around me encircle them.

24. May all generational curses be broken and removed as blessings and peace are born within.

25. May my spirit eye open for protection from the unseen, my spirit ears open to hear the unheard, and that my words be of peace and tranquility.

26. Remove all persons from my life who are not in goodness and love, heal all wounds.

27. Open my heart so that hearts may open to me.

28. I request the Universe to accept the chaos surrounding me and send Angels of Serenity and Peace to guide me.

29. As I inhale, I take in God energy to enlighten my body and revive my soul.

30. My soul anchors my flesh to this realm while my spirit connects me to the Universe.

31. I am a vessel in a man-made world, but my connection with spirit makes me complete.

32. My words, my thoughts, my decisions; release all not guided by spirit.

33. Remove time and life becomes eternal.